W9-AAV-657

Nov. 2019

The Slot Swing

The Proven Way to Hit Consistent and Powerful Shots Like the Pros

Jim McLean

Illustrations by Phil Franké

WILEY

John Wiley & Sons, Inc.

This book is printed on acid-free paper. ∞

Copyright © 2009 by Jim McLean. All rights reserved

Published by John Wiley & Sons, Inc., Hoboken, New Jersey
Published simultaneously in Canada

Illustrations copyright © 2009 by Phil Franké. All rights reserved

No part of this publication may be reproduced, stored in a retrieval system, or transmitted in any form or by any means, electronic, mechanical, photocopying, recording, scanning, or otherwise, except as permitted under Section 107 or 108 of the 1976 United States Copyright Act, without either the prior written permission of the Publisher, or authorization through payment of the appropriate per-copy fee to the Copyright Clearance Center, 222 Rosewood Drive, Danvers, MA 01923, (978) 750–8400, fax (978) 646–8600, or on the web at www.copyright.com. Requests to the Publisher for permission should be addressed to the Permissions Department, John Wiley & Sons, Inc., 111 River Street, Hoboken, NJ 07030, (201) 748–6011, fax (201) 748–6008, or online at http://www.wiley.com/go/permissions.

Limit of Liability/Disclaimer of Warranty: While the publisher and the author have used their best efforts in preparing this book, they make no representations or warranties with respect to the accuracy or completeness of the contents of this book and specifically disclaim any implied warranties of merchantability or fitness for a particular purpose. No warranty may be created or extended by sales representatives or written sales materials. The advice and strategies contained herein may not be suitable for your situation. You should consult with a professional where appropriate. Neither the publisher nor the author shall be liable for any loss of profit or any other commercial damages, including but not limited to special, incidental, consequential, or other damages.

For general information about our other products and services, please contact our Customer Care Department within the United States at (800) 762–2974, outside the United States at (317) 572–3993 or fax (317) 572–4002.

Wiley also publishes its books in a variety of electronic formats. Some content that appears in print may not be available in electronic books. For more information about Wiley products, visit our web site at www.wiley.com.

Library of Congress Cataloging-in-Publication Data:

McLean, Jim, date.
  The slot swing : the proven way to hit consistent and powerful shots like the pros / Jim McLean.
     p. cm.
  ISBN 978-0-470-44499-3 (cloth : alk. paper)
  1. Swing (Golf) I. Title.
  GV979.S9M328 2009
  796.352'3—dc22
                                                                                        2009006818

Printed in the United States of America

10 9 8 7 6 5 4 3 2

To all the golfers with all the different swing shapes. We all know there is one perfect swing. There is a perfect slot.

—Jim McLean

To the incredible ladies in my life: my daughters, Kelly and Colleen; my sister, Maribeth; my best friend and partner, Colleen; and, of course, my mom. I love you all.

—Phil Franké

Contents

Preface

Despite the myriad swings you see on the course and at every level of play, there are only three basic ways to maneuver your clubs back and through to impact. This book focuses on these three swing shapes and how and why each one can work, and it delivers a blueprint to generating crisp, piercing irons and longer drives. The key, as you'll learn, is to find the correct "Slot" on your downswing, no matter how you take the club away in your backswing. The motions are proven and, unlike the majority of golf methods, allow you to make your most natural and athletic swing and build a powerful and repeating motion.

This is my tenth book. *The Slot Swing* attempts to provide you with crucial information in a clear, easy-to-understand format. That's why I've included more than seventy amazing illustrations by Phil Franké, an accomplished artist who has spent decades drawing eye-catching imagery of the swing and its key components. In my opinion, Phil's illustrations bring *The Slot Swing* to life; each one is truly worth a thousand words. In the end, however, I can only present information. It's up to you to get into it, absorb it, and, ultimately, understand it.

In my thirty-five years of teaching golf, I've learned that telling a student something about his swing doesn't mean he understands what I'm talking about. Even when I point out a singular swing key and give him a crystal-clear explanation, I can't guarantee that the information will sink in.

It's one of the reasons golfers continually make the same mistakes, even after they've been told to do it another way. In order to make a positive change in your swing, you must experience the change physically. You have to actually *feel* the change.

And this is a key reason that I think *The Slot Swing* is different. Although you may not fully understand the secrets of the Slot, you're going to clearly see how each of the three swing techniques work, which will help you select the best and most natural model for your game. You will *see* how to get into the Slot and then, hopefully, *feel* it.

I prefer that my students understand clearly what they're trying to do, and I'd be over the moon if I only had to say something once during a lesson and the problem was fixed forever. But it just doesn't work that way. It almost always takes more effort, and nothing is better than a clear visual image.

At first, you may not feel or sense the conceptual and physical differences in your swing after applying the principles of the Slot. It will take some time and often some exaggeration of the key moves for you to actually achieve the results you desire. But by reading this book, you'll realize—maybe for the first time—what you should be doing to achieve the correct delivery line into impact, and this is one of the true fundamentals to ball-striking improvement.

When you go to the range, you'll have a purpose: grooving the new feeling the Slot Swing provides. I've always said that most people go to the driving range not knowing where they are or where they want to go. You'll have a huge leg up on those players. The reason for this is simple: the Slot Swing is all about controlling the position of the shaft, and up until now, the shaft has probably been controlling you.

Acknowledgments

The idea of *The Slot Swing* required drawings to illustrate the three basic swing shapes. I knew I needed great illustrations, and that's when I called Phil Franké, who embodies a fantastic modern touch in his drawing skills. Plus, he is one of the most enthusiastic people I've ever met. Thankfully, he jumped on board.

The illustrations in this book are a huge key to understanding the Slot Swing. In fact, this book is one you hardly have to read—simply study the drawings. They are more effective than words. Thanks to Phil and his talents, I've been able to tell a story I've wanted to tell the golfing public for many years.

It was Phil who drove to New Jersey several times to meet with Stephen Power from John Wiley & Sons, and he also brought in David DeNunzio to help organize and edit this book. I owe all three of these people a debt of gratitude for their great work. I also want to thank one of my master instructors, Joey Wuertenberger, for his tireless efforts in helping me complete this book. Joey is one of the top teachers at the Jim McLean Golf Center in Fort Worth, Texas. He is a phenomenal talent and a dedicated worker. I couldn't have finished this project without Joey pushing me down the homestretch. I also want to thank my current assistant, Eric Lillibridge, who has put in countless hours of time working on this project.

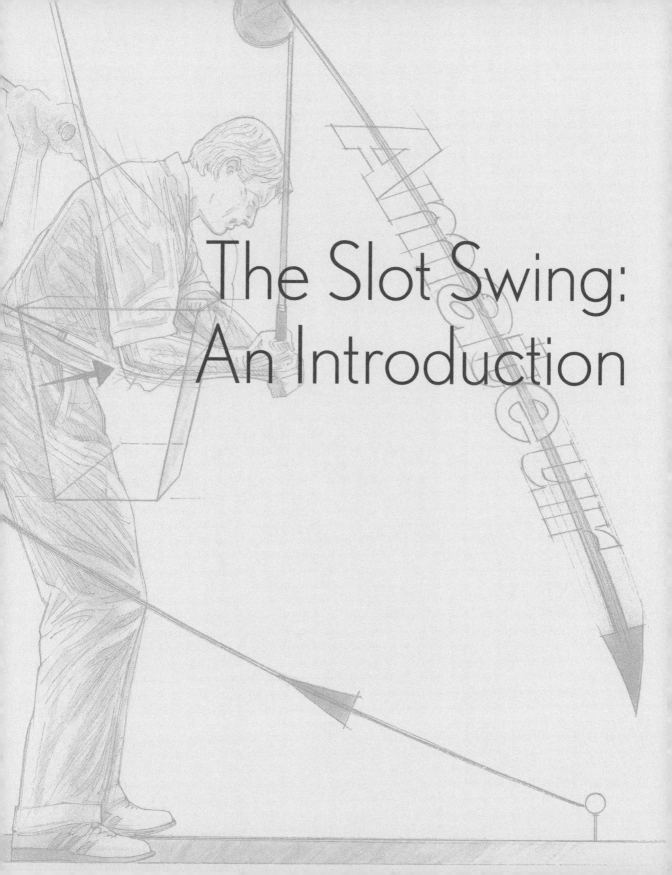

The Slot Swing: An Introduction

One of my goals as an instructor is to demystify the swing: analyze its key parts and break them down and make them easy to understand so that you can incorporate the necessary moves into your technique quickly and with minimal effort. Thanks to digital high-speed photography and video and the advent of sophisticated swing-analysis software, the goal is easier to accomplish—I can see things that previous generations of instructors could only guess about. It's an exciting time in swing study, evaluation, and assessment.

Of course, high-tech machinery helps only to a point. In the end, you have to know what you're looking for. In fact, I made one of my most important discoveries—the one you'll read about in this book—with just an old TV and a pen. A computer? The most advanced piece of equipment in my office at that time was a calculator.

The year was 1980. My research partner, Carl Welty, had devised a way to analyze Tour-player and amateur swings on videotape (which, at the time, was a breakthrough technology itself). Carl had spent years filming—first using an 8mm camera and later a video recorder—almost every Tour player during West Coast Swing events (he's now based in Palm Springs, California), and he owned the most complete library of professional swings on tape. If a player agreed (and not many refused back then), Carl, camera in hand, was at the ready. He was relentless, and we spent hundreds of hours playing, fast-forwarding, and reversing tape, looking for clues, answers, and the hidden secrets to high-level swings. We watched and compared virtually every PGA Tour professional, frame-by-frame, from very exact camera angles.

One of Carl's tricks was to make marks on the TV screen with a dry-erase pen at different points in the swing. (I know it sounds elementary, but believe me, nobody had ever done this before. It was the first baby step toward the computer-driven 3-D programs we use today.) Carl's main interest was in the path the clubhead took from address, to the top, and then back down. I was inclined to study the position of the shaft; how it leaned at address, the angle it made at different points in the backswing and the downswing, and how players controlled it at the top and at impact. Mark. Erase. Mark. Erase. Within months, we had exploded a number of myths commonly held about the swing and had generated a few eyebrow-raising observations.

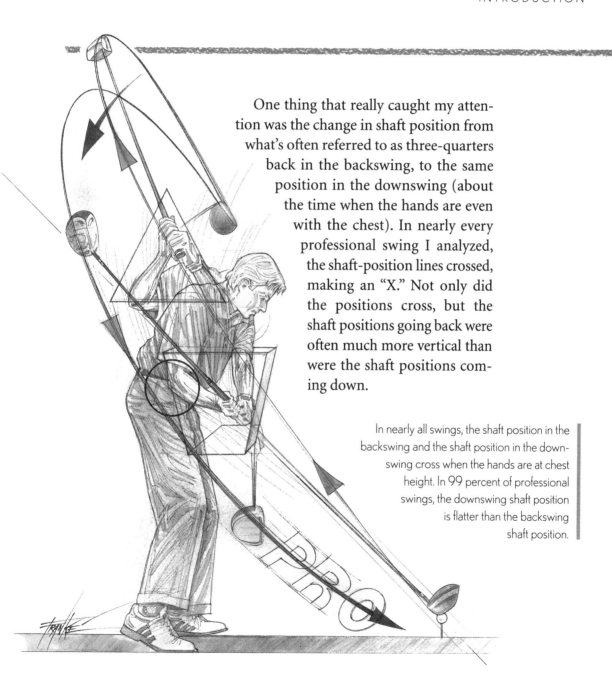

One thing that really caught my attention was the change in shaft position from what's often referred to as three-quarters back in the backswing, to the same position in the downswing (about the time when the hands are even with the chest). In nearly every professional swing I analyzed, the shaft-position lines crossed, making an "X." Not only did the positions cross, but the shaft positions going back were often much more vertical than were the shaft positions coming down.

In nearly all swings, the shaft position in the backswing and the shaft position in the downswing cross when the hands are at chest height. In 99 percent of professional swings, the downswing shaft position is flatter than the backswing shaft position.

A few instructors had preached flattening out the shaft on the downswing, but here was the proof. Visible proof. Catalogued proof. Yet it really told only half of the story. Thankfully, Carl and I also had hundreds of our students' swings on videotape—swings just like yours. We studied these as well. The problem was that most of the amateurs we studied didn't come close to achieving the same shaft action. In fact, many of the amateurs' clubshafts crossed in the opposition direction!

In numerous high-handicap amateur swings that we analyzed, the shaft position at the three-quarters position going back was flatter than the shaft position at the same point coming down—the exact opposite of the positions featured in professional swings. This is the instructional equivalent of finding the Holy Grail: earmarking moves pros make that amateurs don't.

I spoke on the change in shaft position and the research I did with Carl at various PGA seminars throughout the 1980s. It was my original "X," coming long before the now-famous X-Factor cover story on shoulder and hip turn that I wrote for the December 1992 issue of *GOLF* magazine. I mentioned it in my 1996 book, *The X-Factor*, and have incorporated it into the lesson plans we use at each of my schools. This is the first time I've devoted an entire book to the subject, however, because I believe some modern instruction theories are doing golfers like you a bit of a disservice. Several well-known methods promote a one-plane swing and use the Iron Byron machine, with its theoretically "perfect swing," as a model for

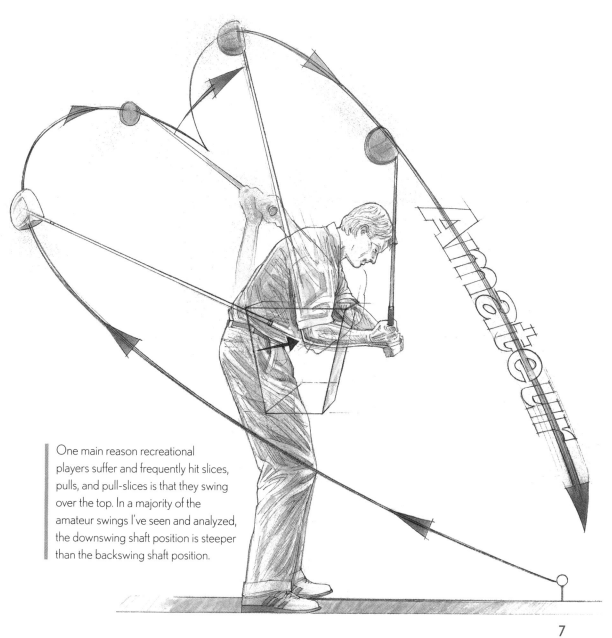

One main reason recreational players suffer and frequently hit slices, pulls, and pull-slices is that they swing over the top. In a majority of the amateur swings I've seen and analyzed, the downswing shaft position is steeper than the backswing shaft position.

you to copy. The problem is that very few great players swing straight up and down on a single plane. There's always a plane shift from backswing to downswing. Not many players ever achieve perfectly matching back and down planes.

The basic element of my shaft-position research is that the shaft swings on one plane going back and on another one coming back down. I'm sure you've heard a lot about one-plane swings, and maybe you've given the idea of swinging on one plane some thought. I wrote this book to clear the air and show you that there's more than one plane to your swing and that it can be much more natural and powerful to change planes than to stay on the same one. (It might seem counter-intuitive, but please read on.)

One way to visualize the swing is to establish a perfect backswing plane and then match it on your downswing. This can be a great way to improve your motion. This book, however, focuses on how to change planes so that your shaft positions cross just as the pros' do. This book shows you how to flatten out your shaft during your downswing, just like Ben Hogan, Byron Nelson, Jack Nicklaus, Lee Trevino, Nick Price, Lorena Ochoa, Jim Furyk, Tiger Woods, Camilo Villegas, Sergio Garcia, and Anthony Kim, among others. It also presents an alternative method that has worked for many accomplished players, including golf greats such as Bobby Jones, Bobby Locke, Hale Irwin, Bernhard Langer, Cory Pavin, Bruce Lietzke, and Sam Snead.

Most important, this book teaches you the one move that makes it all happen: finding the Slot.

1

The Slot Swing
Blueprint

Two important elements define the Slot Swing and make the whole thing work:

1. Your shaft position flattens in your downswing and finds the most effective delivery line to the ball.

2. You change your shaft position by dropping into the Slot after you complete your backswing.

There are three ways to do this, which comprise the three Slot Swings covered in this book. (It'll be up to you to experiment with each and decide which is the best model for you to copy.) These swings share a common trait, in that they train you to change your downswing shaft position and achieve the power-rich delivery line featured in all high-level swings.

The Slot position is the fundamental downswing key to hitting successful shots. When you find it, you have the best chance to release the club freely and generate solid contact, a penetrating ball flight, and the correct trajectory for the club you're holding in your hands. It's the perfect place from which to deliver a centered blow with speed and via the correct angle of attack.

Remember: a perfect swing is one that repeats. It's one that is powerful and accurate and, most important, works under pressure. That's why this book emphasizes finding the Slot more than it does finding perfect backswings. Making a perfect backswing doesn't mean you'll be perfect at impact. The proof is simple—just look at the greatest ball-strikers in history. Examine the swings that have lasted. Think about the swings that stand the test of time. They all find the Slot.

The Slot Swing: How It Works

So far, I've mentioned the word *plane* several times. Specifically, I've described the main element of the Slot Swing as a switch from a backswing plane to a flatter downswing plane. The question begs, then, "What's the best plane?" Whenever I'm asked, I'm tempted to answer, "Delta" or "Continental," because there isn't one—at least, where your golf swing is concerned. Watch any professional tournament on TV, and you'll see in an instant that the ideal backswing plane differs from golfer to golfer. The concept gets really complicated when you consider that each of the clubs in your bag is built with a unique lie angle and that you swing them on different slopes.

If you're like most golfers, you're intimidated by plane. I don't blame you; discussions on the topic are vague and incomplete. Over the years, you've been misled by the oft-used illustration depicting swing plane as a shadowed area (typically, a sheet of glass) that rests on your shoulders. Despite the good intentions of this graphic, it doesn't tell you anything about the plane on which you start your swing, just the one at the midpoint in your backswing (and mainly for your lead arm). Your swing begins on an "address plane," defined by the angle formed by the shaft when you sole your clubhead on the ground. The address plane is many degrees flatter than the sheet of glass. Obviously, something has to happen in order for you to change from the lower address plane to the higher backswing plane as you power the club to the top. Look at the swing diagrams of our representative professionals in this book, and you'll clearly see that the hands veer upward in a curving path at the start of the backswing, leaving the lower plane and rising to the one that slices through your shoulders. There are exceptions, but this is nonetheless a solid observation.

The same goes for your downswing, but here you need to change from a higher plane to a lower plane. Often, when an amateur initially attempts this, he tries to track the move he made going back. That's not how it works. Your hands don't re-track on the way back down to the ball. They remain on the same plane they rest on at the top (or get slightly steeper). It's the *clubshaft* that falls to the lower plane (finds the Slot), a move that happens naturally when you trigger your downswing by shifting your lower-body center toward the target (more on that in chapter 3).

It's important to realize that the act of swinging "on plane" doesn't mean that your hands, left arm, and shaft work in the same plane at the same time. Although there are some points in your swing where everything matches up, it's incredibly difficult to plane everything perfectly, including the clubhead, the shaft, the hands, and the arms. While it might look good on paper or to a scientist, achieving perfect positions is incredibly difficult and unnatural. It doesn't correspond to an athletic throwing motion or hitting mechanics. Trying to be perfect usually leads to overthinking, freezing up, and, at times, quitting the game.

The best thing about the Slot Swing is that it doesn't care about your exact backswing plane. As you'll learn, it won't matter what plane you take as you swing the club to the top or what plane your club sits on when you get there. I've built in several Safety Corridors that, in essence, demand that you simply get within a range. The only plane of extreme importance is the one you shift your clubshaft onto at the start of your downswing.

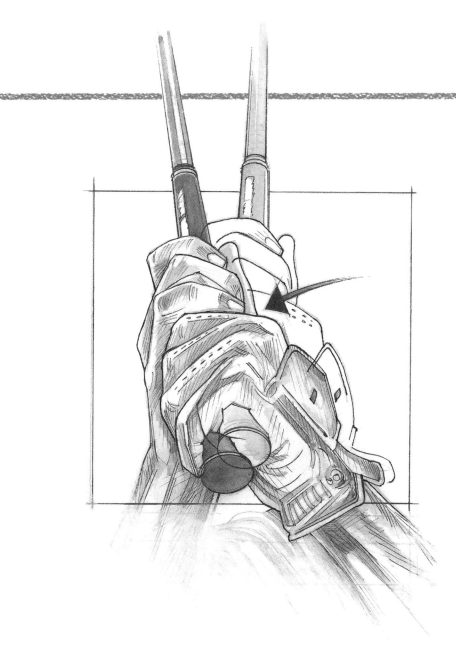

Your hands don't re-track on the way back down to the ball.
They remain on the same plane they rest on at the top (or get
slightly steeper). It's the *clubshaft* that falls to the lower plane.

15

Slot Swing 1: The Standard Slot Swing

In the first and most common Slot Swing, your club tracks above the address plane during your backswing, then *drops* at the start of your downswing and does so in such a way that your shaft position instantly flattens out (or becomes less vertical than the shaft position established at the three-quarters position in your backswing). Sergio Garcia's swing is a good example of this type of Slot Swing. As you'll read, dropping into the Slot as Sergio does by flattening the shaft on the downswing requires the least amount of effort on your part, which is why it's the type of Slot Swing that I recommend many of my students follow.

Sergio Garcia's inside loop
Standard Slot Swing.

Slot Swing 2: The Reverse Slot Swing

The second type of Slot Swing is a reverse of the first, which is why I call it the Reverse Slot Swing. The clubhead swings inside during the takeaway and under the shaft plane in a way that could be described as "flat." A Reverse Slot swinger—Sam Snead is a good example—makes an early turn in the backswing and positions his right arm and elbow well behind his body. Starting down, the hands and the arms loop well outward to get everything lined up. The clubhead trails the hands, instead of tipping over in front of the body: a classic death move. As you'll discover, the Reverse Slot is probably the most natural way to swing a club.

Sam Snead's Reverse
Slot Swing.

19

Slot Swing 3: The "Single-Plane" Slot Swing

The third type of Slot Swing mimics the type of motion that you see Tiger Woods work on. It's the most technically perfect model swing and the Slot Swing that most closely follows the one-plane swing method, which, in my opinion, is the most difficult swing to repeat consistently. Trying to swing on one plane sounds easy, but it actually requires the most athleticism and requires you to be perfect at almost every position in your motion. That takes years of work. Plus, most golfers who think they swing on one plane actually change planes.

Nevertheless, the single-plane shape is the best visual for most young golfers and beginners, and that's why it merits attention when we discuss the Slot. A single plane is easy to comprehend and is an excellent teaching concept to help the student understand that the swing is a circular motion (a circle lying on its side).

Whether you flatten your shaft in your downswing by using the Standard or the Reverse Slot Swing, or try to follow the principles of the Single-Plane Slot, this book will help you find the perfect downswing position that every pro hits and most amateurs miss. Dropping into the Slot overwhelms you with confidence, so much so that you'll have zero desire to make any compensating moves as you approach the ball. The club feels lighter and—maybe for the first time—totally under your control. When you hear a Tour professional say, "My swing felt really good today" after completing a competitive round, what he's really saying is that he was in the Slot.

Three Shapes of the Slot Swing

The "Standard" Slot Swing

Sergio Garcia: Garcia's arms and club-shaft start out and away from the body. He has great width in the takeaway with the clubshaft well above the plane going back. At the top, the clubshaft falls dramatically backward, however, then drops down into the slot, and the clubhead approaches the ball from a perfect on-line delivery.

The "Sing

Tiger Woods:
original plan
swing. His
slot, ther
Tiger
the

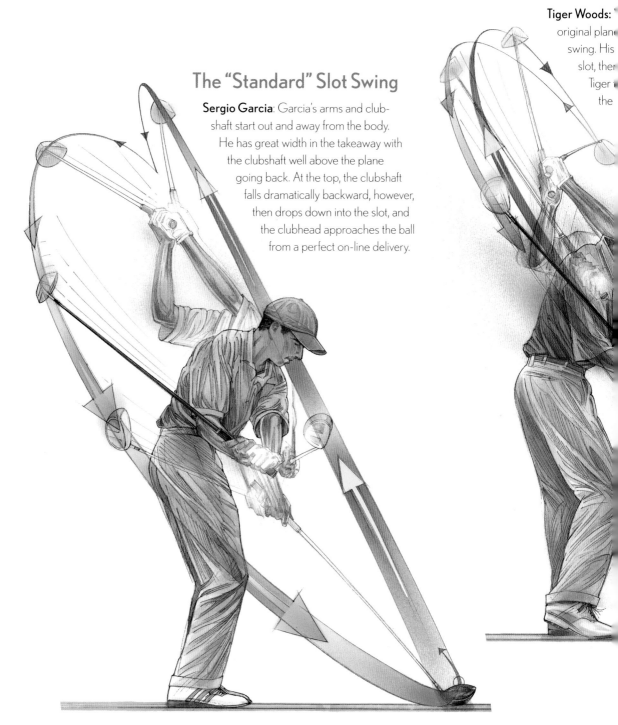

le Plane" Slot Swing

Woods takes the club away parallel to the shaft's
, his goal to match this plane shaft on the down-
s a true one-plane swing, coming up out of the
returning to it on the way down.
ies to have his left arm and
club match up, too.

The "Reverse" Slot Swing

Bruce Lietzke: In the classic sledgehammer
move, Lietzke's arms and clubshaft move in and
under the plane at takeaway, he makes an early
body coil, then his arms and clubshaft loop to
the outside. But coming down the clubshaft
finds the slot, and Lietzke winds up in a classic
delivery position.

Tiger Woods's Single-Plane
Slot Swing.

21

The Slot is a position and a feeling. You find the Slot when you flatten your clubshaft position in your downswing so that the clubhead attacks the ball from the correct angle inside the target line. In a classic Slot Swing, you move from a steep position in your backswing to a flatter, more horizontal position in your downswing.

22

The Slot: Why It's Good for Your Game

We see every kind of swing the human body can make every day at my golf schools, and I'm fully aware of the latest teaching methods designed to make them better (or at least become more consistent). Some of these teaching methods are very good. Some are suspect. The better methods all fit into the McLean Safety Corridors, which my instructors teach at our schools. A good majority of them are designed for the advanced or professional player, but they are often very capable of causing more damage than good when applied to an amateur's swing.

That's the big difference between the Slot Swing and other methods touted in magazines, on Web sites, and on TV: the Slot Swing is designed to improve the swings of recreational golfers (i.e., you). Although we'll use professionals such as Sergio Garcia and Jim Furyk to demonstrate how the Slot works, it's still something the average weekend golfer can learn to improve his game. As you read through this book, you'll discover how the simple moves that make up the act of slotting the club in your downswing can

- Give you more freedom in your swing (instead of asking you to follow a strict diet of positions and angles).

- Make it much easier to approach the ball from inside the target line (the path opposite the one that causes your slice).
- Improve your rhythm and tempo.
- Add power to your tee shots and to each of your irons.

Plus, the Slot Swing eliminates the most damaging swing error you can make: coming over the top.

Coming over the top is a move made by many amateurs who visit my golf schools. Even as I watch players tee off on one of the courses here at Doral Golf Resort, I see mostly over-the-top after over-the-top swing. Very rarely will an amateur slot the club and approach the ball properly from inside the target line. It's a serious issue and likely the single greatest roadblock between the player you are and the player you deserve to be.

Swinging over the top—with its resultant slices, pulls, pull-slices, and tops—usually happens when you take the club back too far to the inside (toward your body) and then swing the club outside the target line and steep on your downswing and cut across the ball through impact. As hard as you try to stop swinging over the top, you can't.

You know you're coming over the top if

- You tend to hit a lot of slices.
- Your divots point well left of your target.
- You make contact out near the toe.
- Your divots are deep, often toe deep.

wide open

NO

YES

Whipping the club to the inside—a death move and a precursor to coming over the top.

The only solace you can take if you come over the top is that so many other golfers are doing it, too. It's one big reason handicaps fail to drop and is something most modern swing fixes don't address.

One of the first things I show a student who's plagued by an over-the-top swing is a video of Jim Furyk, Sergio Garcia, or Miller Barber—the same examples I'll show you in this book. Invariably, the student is confused: "How am I supposed to copy a Tour player?" The answer is easy: you're not copying the swing, but rather the inside loop.

The inside Slot move requires the least amount of athleticism and has the greatest margin for error. Plus, when you do it correctly, it makes it almost impossible to come over the top. You don't need perfect backswing positions. You just need to get the shaft more vertical and then one good move at the start of your downswing that causes your clubshaft to flatten out and approach the ball from inside the target line.

With the Slot Swing, slicing is difficult. Hitting powerful shots that draw toward the target are far more likely.

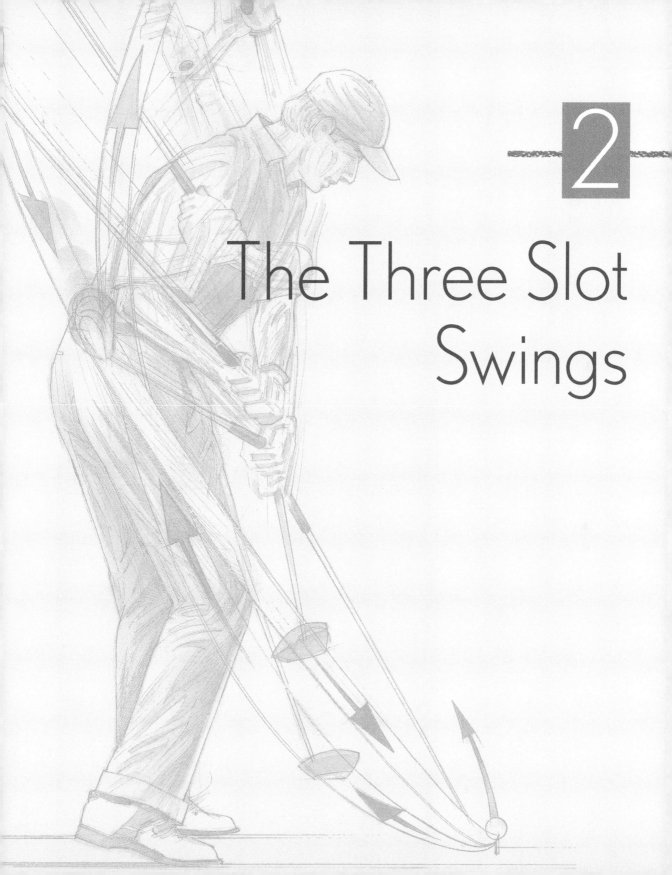

The Three Slot Swings

2

The Slot is a moment in time—a link between the plane your shaft travels on during your backswing to the one it assumes as you deliver the clubhead into the back of the ball. Finding it automatically turns your swing into a Slot Swing and, like most other elements of the Slot, allows for a ton of freedom in your motion. There's no greater evidence of this than the fact that you can use any one of three swings to hit the Slot and power the ball as you've never done before.

The main difference between each Slot Swing is how you take the club to the top—either above the address plane, below it, or on it. The differences disappear on the way back down, with a series of important moves that transition the shaft to the most effective delivery line into impact. This line is the same, regardless of which Slot Swing you adopt, and it's the one shared by any great ball-striker who has ever lived.

The Standard Slot Swing

Swinging the club slightly above the plane line and setting the shaft on a steeper backswing plane, then lowering it to a flatter downswing plane, is the easiest way for most golfers to hit quality shots consistently. That's why I most frequently recommend the Slot Swing to my students and why it's so prominently featured in this book. There are golfers who fare better with the Reverse Slot and Single-Plane Slot Swings, but for the majority, finding the Slot by getting the backswing plane more vertical and then shifting the club-shaft onto a flatter plane at the start of their downswing will make the quickest, most dramatic, long-term improvement in their game.

The moves that cause the Slot to happen are found in 99 percent of professional swings, both past and present. (Long before Byron Nelson stuck a steel shaft into a clubhead, hickory-stick players used the Slot, too.) In researching the Slot over the years, I've selected three professionals who most accurately display the powerful dynamics of the Slot. What's interesting is that these players reach the Slot position in very different ways. Although we'll explore the Slot Swing, position by position, in chapter 4, looking at these three players' techniques is a great way to get an idea of how the Standard Slot works and the freedom it allows in your motion.

Slot Swing Exhibit A: Miller Barber

Miller Barber is a world-class touring professional with thirty-five victories under his belt, of which twenty-four were claimed on the Champions Tour (formerly the Senior Tour). Miller is third on the all-time Champions Tour victory list, behind only Lee Trevino and Hale Irwin. Five of Miller's twenty-four victories on the Senior Tour were Majors. He was also considered one of golf's finest ball-strikers for fifty years.

What's more interesting about Miller Barber than all of his victories is his swing. If you've ever seen it, you'd be hard-pressed to imagine him holding a championship trophy, let alone thirty-five of them. In fact, Jackie Burke, the hall-of-fame player and one of my biggest mentors, once said of Barber's swing, "It looks like an octopus falling out of a tree." Others have quipped that it reminds them of a man trying to open an umbrella in a hurricane. You get the idea.

Without question, Barber's swing is easily identifiable. He takes the club away well to the outside of the target line and lifts it almost straight into the air with the clubface dead shut.

His right elbow flies, and his left arm becomes nearly vertical. Once he starts his downswing, however, he makes one of the all-time great loops back to the inside. He changes the orientation of his clubshaft by approximately five feet and drops it right into the Slot. In his own words, Barber says of his technique, "After I loop the club to the inside on my downswing, I look like any good player. The downswing is what matters."

Even the most untrained eye can see that Barber takes the club away to the outside of the plane line on his backswing. As he does, his clubface closes and his elbows disconnect from his body, while he lifts the shaft into the air as if he's trying to squash a bug on a ten-foot ceiling. When he reaches the top of the backswing, his left arm is very upright and his hands are well above the top of his head, setting the club almost perpendicular to the ground. Even Miller's posture straightens up as he loses his original spine angle.

Basically, Barber breaks almost every backswing rule in the book. He's in a position that most teachers would change. But once he transitions to his downswing, things fall into place. He transforms from toad into prince. The ugliness is over, and the beauty begins. He finds the Slot.

How does he do it? First, he drops his arms, elbows, and hands straight down—not toward the ball—much in the same way that a baseball player drops his bat as the pitch comes to the plate. As everything drops, the shaft dips below his right shoulder, and by the time the club reaches the

Despite taking the club back well to the outside and lifting it high over his head, Miller Barber earned a reputation as perhaps the most solid ball-striker of his generation. His secret? A looping move at the start of his downswing that dropped the club into the Slot—a move that he could easily repeat.

delivery position, Barber's swing looks as good as anyone's. You would never know that the club had taken such a crazy ride from the start to just before impact.

Ben Hogan once advised Barber to work on building a repeating swing (and not changing his backswing), and, for all its quirks and idiosyncrasies, he did. It never changed, and it always packed a tremendous punch. To a man, the players of his era conclude that Miller Barber hit the ball more solidly than anyone on Tour.

Slot Swing Exhibit B: Sergio Garcia

Sergio Garcia flashed onto the professional scene at the young age of nineteen. For the last ten years, he has been a bright spot on Tour with his engaging personality and eye-popping power. He's one of the top ball-strikers in the world, with ten international victories and seven PGA Tour wins. During his career, he's led the PGA Tour in Total Driving, Greens in Regulation, and Total Ballstriking.

Garcia's swing produces some of the most piercing and accurate shots on Tour, especially with his irons. He's known for smashing the ball hard, yet maintaining control of its flight. Personally, I can attest to these claims. When the PGA Tour makes its annual wintertime stop at Doral Golf Resort here in Miami, I spend hours observing Sergio, both on the practice tee and on the course.

Sergio Garcia owns one of the most unique swings on Tour, and it's a classic Slot Swing. He traces a very wide backswing arc, holds off the hinging action of his wrists, and positions his left arm very high with the clubshaft laid off (pointing left of the target) at the top. Then he shifts the shaft to a significantly flatter plane by dropping his hands straight down and attaching his right elbow to his right hip during the first half of his downswing. Like Ben Hogan and Lee Trevino before him, Garcia flattens the clubshaft to the maximum. When I show students his swing, they can't believe how flat, narrow, and behind the body Sergio sets his clubshaft on his downswing.

Unlike Miller Barber, Garcia takes the club halfway back on what most teachers would describe as above the ideal plane. At the halfway-back position, his arms are "long" and his wrists have barely hinged, creating the widest swing plane possible. As he continues back, his wrists eventually break, and they do so in a way that sets the club in a laid-off position (pointing left of target).

During the club's journey to the top, Sergio makes a great and powerful shoulder turn, slides his weight slightly outside his right foot, and bows his right knee outward—a few more things that many teachers would change. But hopefully by now you're getting the idea: many backswing taboos have zero negative impact on the ability to hit great shots when you find the Slot.

Sergio's first move from the top is to drop his hands straight down. He increases the hinge in his wrists tremendously, taking his swing arc from very wide in the backswing to very narrow on the way back down. His shaft flattens and becomes even more laid off. He finds the Slot, generating incredible clubhead lag and tons of energy that he uses to hammer the ball.

One of the things that Garcia does so well—which is paramount to the Slot Swing—is dropping his right elbow down at the start of his downswing. Dropping the right elbow toward your right hip is key, but if you watch Sergio, you'll see that his arms and club drop in response to the initial movement of his lower body. (It's important to understand that a Slot swinger like Sergio triggers his downswing by moving his lower body to the left, not by throwing his arms at the ball.) When he reaches the halfway-down point, his right elbow appears to be "glued" to his right hip. Now he can pull the trigger and fire everything he's got through impact for a powerful hit. Sergio is an extreme example of slotting the club with strength.

Slot Swing Exhibit C: Jim Furyk

Jim Furyk is well known for his unorthodox swing. If most golf instructors had gotten their hands on Jim's swing during his younger years, there's a good chance you'd never have heard of him (and I wouldn't be writing about him). Jim receives swing instruction only from his father, and it's been that way his entire life.

From more than thirty years of research, I can tell you that many of the world's best players, such as Jim, posses unique swing characteristics, especially on the backswing. In the end, these individual qualities don't affect how well they play. One of my early mentors, Claude Harmon, loved to say that he could "make eight loops at the top of my backswing and still hit great shots." He also said, "It's not how you back the car out of the garage that counts."

Furyk has eleven PGA Tour victories, including the 2003 U.S. Open Championship. He's finished in the top 5 on the Tour money list four times in the last twelve years and competed in four Ryder Cups and four President Cups. In 2005,

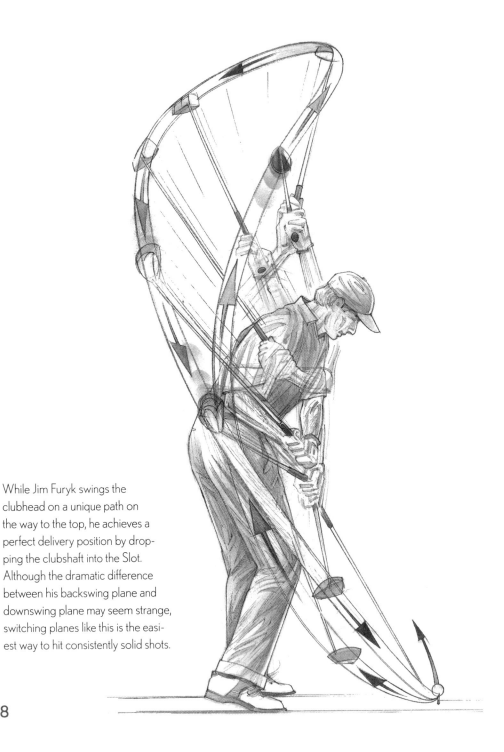

While Jim Furyk swings the clubhead on a unique path on the way to the top, he achieves a perfect delivery position by dropping the clubshaft into the Slot. Although the dramatic difference between his backswing plane and downswing plane may seem strange, switching planes like this is the easiest way to hit consistently solid shots.

Furyk finished third in Scoring Average (69.27), fourth on the money list, and seventh in Greens in Regulation (69.8 percent). Currently, he's fourth on the Tour's career earnings list, with $34 million dollars. And he's a Slot swinger.

During Furyk's takeaway, notice how he swings the club back just a little to the inside. (Miller Barber takes it back outside, and Sergio Garcia takes it back on plane.) Furyk's hands and arms definitely dominate his initial move away from the ball. After the club passes the halfway-back position, the club suddenly peels off into an extremely upright path. His club finally arrives at the top of his backswing in an overly vertical and steep position (similar to Miller Barber's).

As Furyk begins his downswing, he re-routes his arms, hands, and club dramatically. In fact, milliseconds after reaching the top, his swing suddenly changes shape. His shaft flattens, and his arms and hands fall into place.

Whereas Sergio keeps his right elbow glued to his right hip in the delivery position, Furyk sets his right elbow *behind* his right hip. Although I don't recommend this extreme inside position, it works for Furyk and, at its base level, is further evidence that the clubshaft shifts to a flatter position in high-level swings and is additional proof that good players keep their right elbows close to or alongside their right hips on the downswing. This is a result of the arms and the club dropping from a high position at the top of the backswing and staying slightly behind the turning action of the body during the downswing.

Jim Furyk is an elite golfer with Hall-of-Fame credentials. He's also a poster child for the Slot and its amazing ability to generate crisp, powerful shots from a not-so-pretty swing.

The Reverse Slot

The most natural move in the world for a golfer to make is to power the club to the inside on the takeaway and then loop the hands and the arms forward on the downswing, which, if done correctly, can effectively slot the club. This is the basis of the second Slot Swing, the Reverse Slot.

The difference between a Reverse Slot Swing and the one that most amateurs make when they swing their clubs to the inside during the takeaway is that in a Reverse Slot Swing, the club never gets in front of the hands when the club starts down. Unfortunately, most amateur golfers habitually commit this error by moving their shoulders outward from the top and throwing their clubs at the ball in a steep orientation. It's a reaction to the natural "hit impulse" built into every golfer—we're almost designed to swing over the top, with the shaft over the downswing plane and at too steep an angle. I single out amateur players because a junior golfer often makes a similar move with the arms and the shoulders, but since he possesses less strength, the clubshaft falls onto the natural and correct shallow path.

The next time you're at the range, look for a young golfer. Almost every untrained youngster slings the club to the inside on the backswing. The difference between the natural swinging action of a child, however, and your inside move is that a kid winds his hips and shoulders. Almost every adult simply swings the club to the inside with the arms, while the body does almost nothing. From here, the adult throws the club at the ball from the top with as much force as he can muster. This is not good.

Meet Mr. Lietzke

I've known PGA Tour player Bruce Lietzke for nearly forty years. We roomed together at the University of Houston and then traveled together during our early playing days on the mini-tour. Eventually, Bruce became known as the finest ball-striker on the PGA Tour during a career that spanned twenty-eight years. In his prime, he was an absolute money machine. He won at least one Tour event every year for eleven years straight and led the Total Driving category (which combines Driving Distance average and Fairways Hit percentage) nine times. The best way to describe how well Bruce struck the ball was that he once finished in the top 20 in the money category, while ranking dead last in putting average. How well do you have to hit the ball to do that?

Bruce is one of the great professionals who swings the club to the inside and then loops it in the opposite direction at the top. You may not believe it, but this reverse loop slots the club perfectly. If you compared Lietzke's downswing position to Sergio Garcia's, they'd look nearly the same, with the club in the Slot and approaching the ball from the inside.

Bruce and other Reverse Slot swingers feature a hand position at three-quarters back that's noticeably flatter than their hand position coming down. In chapter 1, it may have appeared that I earmarked this as mostly an "amateur move" and the primary cause of slices, pulls, and pull-slices. But Lietzke (and Sam Snead, Bobby Jones, Bobby Locke, Craig Stadler, Raymond Floyd, Craig Perry, Hale Irwin, J. B. Holmes, and Retief Goosen, to name just a few) doesn't break my shaft-position theory. A Reverse Slot player never allows the shaft to "tip over" during the downswing and move in front of his body into a very vertical position, which is the typical amateur mistake.

When I wrote *The X Factor*, I described shaft tip-over (or throwing the clubhead out with the hands) as the classic death move. A Reverse Slot swinger doesn't do that. He loops his hands out with his shoulders without bringing the shaft down on too steep of an angle. As a result, the club finds the Slot.

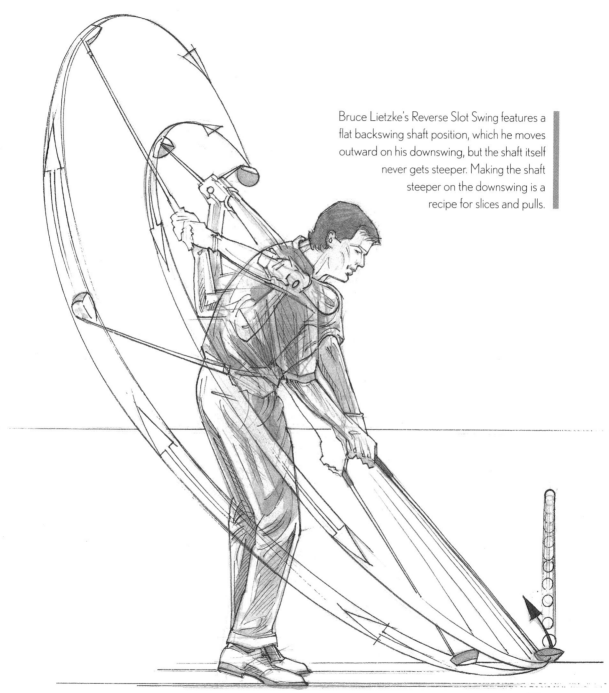

Bruce Lietzke's Reverse Slot Swing features a flat backswing shaft position, which he moves outward on his downswing, but the shaft itself never gets steeper. Making the shaft steeper on the downswing is a recipe for slices and pulls.

43

A good way to think about the Reverse Slot is that it *raises* your shaft from a flat position to a Slot Position, but not a steep position. In other words, your hands and arms loop *up* to find the Slot (compared to dropping down in the Standard Slot Swing). This is the same move that Hall-of-Famer Sam Snead used to bag a record eighty-two PGA Tour wins. Snead's forward loop was as visually obvious as Lietzke's; he lifted his shaft position from a lower plane on his backswing to the Slot plane on his downswing.

A Sledgehammer Swing

Earlier, I used the image of a baseball player swinging a bat to demonstrate how the inside-loop Slot Swing works (and I'll revisit the comparison in chapter 4). The baseball image doesn't really apply to a Reverse Slot swinger. The classic image of swinging a sledgehammer is a better fit.

Although modern machinery has made the act of swinging a sledgehammer nearly obsolete, most people are familiar with the action. You've seen it dozens of times in movies and on TV—the laboring railroad worker driving a spike into a section of railroad track. Take away the railroad and the tumbleweeds and replace the sledgehammer with a driver or a 7-iron, and you have the Reverse Slot.

Because the sledgehammer is heavy, the worker swings the

Sam Snead won more Tour events using a Reverse Slot Swing than any other golfer did. Notice how the shaft plane rises in his downswing. He accomplished this by allowing his right wrist to cup as he looped the club forward at the top. This prevented the club from moving out in front of his body so that it could maintain an extremely power-rich inside track to the ball.

hammer inside, and once he gains momentum, he lifts it up using the big muscles in his shoulders and back. Think about how you move another heavy object, such as a beer keg. You tip it on its bottom edge and roll it. In other words, "you turn weight." That's the easiest and most natural way to move a heavy object.

In order to build momentum and really drive that spike into the rail, the man swinging the sledgehammer loops his hands up and over at the start of his downswing. This is precisely the move that a young junior makes when swinging a club that's a bit too heavy for him. Although his arms and hands loop out away from him, the head of the sledgehammer stays back. It trails the hands. The man driving the spike into the railroad tie never thinks about these moves, but he hits that spike dead center. He never misses.

Think about this: Would a person driving a spike be better off taking the sledgehammer straight up on a perfect plane and then tracing that perfect plane down to the spike? If that were true, don't you think someone would have done it?

The secret to swinging in the Reverse Slot is probably to learn it at an early age. It *is* the most natural way to play golf, yet almost nobody talks about it or teaches it. Many young and promising juniors have potentially been limited because instructors aren't aware that so many great ball-strikers and top professionals swing the club this way. If you have a son or a daughter who wants to learn golf, keep this advice in mind.

The Reverse Slot: A Recommendation

The usefulness of the Reverse Slot cannot be denied. Jack Nicklaus, Gary Player, and Lee Trevino have dubbed Sam Snead's Reverse Slot Swing the greatest swing in the history of the game. Snead won many professional tournaments during the course of six decades—talk about a swing that stood the test of time! He finished second in a regular PGA Tour event when he was sixty-seven years old. In that tournament, he shot his age in three of the four rounds, a feat unheard of in the history of the Tour. Snead also shot 59 ten times (once in a Tour event). Bobby Locke, another Reverse Slot swinger, won five British Opens. Bobby Jones won thirteen majors and the Grand Slam with the Reverse Slot, and Bruce Lietzke used the Reverse Slot to make millions of dollars practically in his spare time in between fishing trips. Lietzke rarely practiced his swing and was the envy of his peers on Tour. The Reverse Slot was an easy, natural swing for these players.

Moreover, the longest drivers of the current generation, John Daly and J. B. Holmes, are Reverse Slot swingers. Obviously, something good can result from reversing the Slot.

My take on the Reverse Slot is that it really is the most natural way to swing a golf club. The players I have listed were all light on range time. They did not grind or think much about their golf swings. The Reverse Slot is a much-overlooked way to play great golf. If executed correctly, it's a fantastic way to hit a golf ball.

The Single-Plane Slot

Many instructors and swing theorists advocate swinging on one plane: they say that the ideal swing creates a perfect plane going back and retraces that exact angle coming back down. In other terms, the clubhead draws a perfect circle back and down. After studying hundreds of high-level players and watching almost 100 percent of them change planes and drop into the Slot from the top of their backswings, I'm hard-pressed to agree with the one-plane technique. Yet I do agree that it's a wonderfully simple idea for visualizing the swing and that it can be very useful in teaching. In fact, I use this basic idea all the time—I just don't require the student to be perfect.

The lure of a single plane is strong. Why make things difficult by changing planes? The answer is that when you flatten your shaft, you turn your club into a whip. By trying to stay perfectly on one plane, it's harder to get that "fall-in" move that happens when you lead your hit (or throw) with your right elbow. When you achieve the fall-in action, you also get the force it generates when your right elbow drops underneath your right hand. Lee Trevino talked passionately about this very move and how it brought his entire swing together. In Lee's terms, "It's to my advantage not to have a perfect swing. I'd rather not have the perfect backswing. It's better to have your own one move you can go with every time to start the downswing."

The perfect swing—like the pot of gold at the end of the rainbow, the Fountain of Youth, and other appealing quests— exists only in our minds. To date, instructors and swing theorists have yet to find any human being with a perfect swing. Even if you take your club back perfectly and set it in perfect position at the top, there's absolutely no guarantee that you're going to be perfect coming down or at impact. A perfect backswing in no way means that you'll hit perfect shots. The research that Carl Welty and I carried out has proved that you must have speed and center contact, must slot the swing starting down, and must have a great path into impact to generate Tour-quality results.

The basic principles of a one-plane swing are excellent, however, for demonstrating the overall shape of the swing. In our schools, we use swing circles to help our students learn that they should swing in a circle, both back and through, and that the circle is tilted, with its base of the circle at the ball and its top approximately at the chest. Combining this thought with the athletic hitting motion inherent in the Slot makes this teaching swing a Single-Plane Slot Swing.

In a Single-Plane Slot Swing, the golfer attempts to trace a circle back and through. But what we really hope happens is that his swing achieves a greater dynamic and the whiplike action needed to hit powerful and strong shots.

Tiger and the Single-Plane Slot

It's obvious by now that Tiger Woods is one of the greatest players of this or any generation. His accomplishments are unparalleled for a golfer his age, and it looks like there's no stopping him. He's one of several players who strive to employ a Single-Plane Slot Swing. If you try to swing this way, it will require dedication beyond what most recreational players can afford. Nevertheless, his is a good swing to look at to confirm the power of the Slot and to recognize that even players who attempt to swing on one plane still might change the downswing plane.

Tiger starts his swing on the original shaft plane, a move he's likely spent hundreds of hours perfecting. But as soon as he reaches the midpoint of his backswing, he raises his hands, arms, and clubshaft to a higher plane. It gives the appearance of a one-plane swing, because his second plane is perfectly parallel to the original address plane. The idea is to line up the left arm, the hands, and the clubshaft on the address plane.

From the top, Tiger—like all Slot swingers—allows his hands, arms, and clubshaft to fall in response to the movement of his lower-body center. He allows them to react, not act. By the time Tiger's hands reach hip height, you'll notice that he looks very much like all of the other golfers we've examined in this book. His impact plane angle is definitely higher than his address plane, further evidence that he starts his swing on one plane and ends at impact on another. Only a few Tour players return the clubshaft back to the original address plane, and none of them are one-plane swingers.

If you look at Tiger's swing, you'll realize just how technically perfect he strives to be. Even though he changes planes, his goal is to stay parallel to a single one. Again, this sort of perfection is years in the making.

The primary benefit of the Slot becomes obvious when you understand that you don't have to be technically perfect on the way up or at the top to look like Tiger in the downswing delivery zone. Your backswing only needs to stay within the Safety Corridors I outlined in chapter 4.

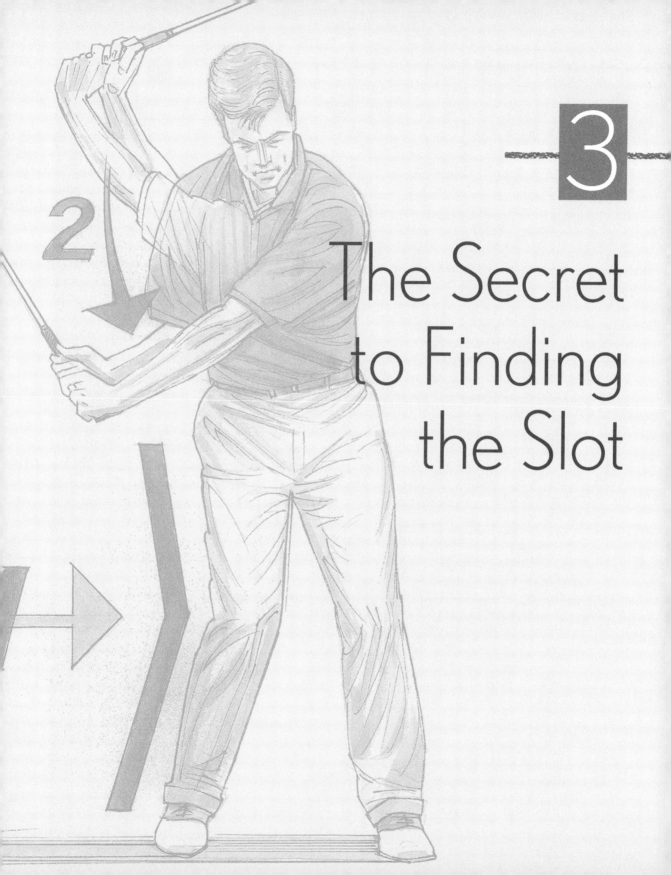

3

The Secret
to Finding
the Slot

If you go back and look at the top-of-the-backswing positions of Miller Barber, Sergio Garcia, and Jim Furyk (or examine photographs of Ben Hogan, Sam Snead, Arnold Palmer, Jack Nicklaus, Bruce Lietzke, Phil Mickelson, Johnny Miller, Tom Watson, Nick Faldo, Corey Pavin, and Lee Trevino, to name just a few), you'll find that each has a different look. Their swing lengths are different, their shaft locations vary, and they each point the clubface in a different direction.

The fact that no two professionals look exactly alike at the top—but look so similar once they get halfway down to impact—gives you an idea of the power of the Slot and how it can fix unorthodox backswing positions so that the clubhead can approach the ball from the inside and

The fact that no two professionals look exactly alike at the top—but look so similar once they get halfway down and then through impact—gives you an idea of the power of the Slot.

transfer all of the energy of your swing into the hit. It's also the power of your first move down from the top, when the Slot takes shape.

Although it's possible to hit good shots without finding the Slot, it requires that you time an infinite number of bad motions and off-plane angles. This is difficult for most amateurs to do on a consistent basis, which explains why they often follow a good shot with a bad one. This type of inconsistency disappears when you learn to find the Slot during your downswing.

It is possible to hit good shots, acceptable shots, and not be in the Slot. You can time an infinite number of bad motions and off-plane angles. It is harder to do, but it does happen.

Over the next few pages, I'll discuss slotting the club and the key moves you must make from the top of your backswing. When you swing in the Slot, there's not much conscious directing or manipulating the club, at least not after you've practiced the Slot motion and can make the move in your practice swings.

Your first move from the top is to shift your lower body laterally toward the target.

59

The Secret Is in the Shift

Regardless of what your top position looks like, your lower body is the first thing to move from the top, and the principles involved in this motion are the same ones you use in every other athletic throwing or hitting motion. These principles are shifting, rotating your body center, and releasing your right arm (for a right-handed golfer). You can't defy the laws of an athletic throw if your goal is to hit the ball far and straight. And once you apply them, you won't have to consciously think about pulling the club downward. (You may feel a pull in your left arm, but that'll only be in response to the force generated by your body turn. Correct body actions ensure that the arms whip the club powerfully into impact from the inside so that the center of your clubface makes contact with the back of the ball.)

This means that the first move down—the first act in slotting the club in your downswing—is a "below-the-belt" event. Almost immediately on finishing your backswing, get your lower body moving toward the target. Lee Trevino always said that he liked to "break my knees toward the target" to start his downswing. That's one good way to capture the correct feel. As you shift your knees forward, moving your weight along with them, allow the triangle formed by your elbows and arms (see "Top of the Backswing" in chapter 4) to drop down. If you do it correctly, the clubshaft will be trailing and, due to the forward action of your lower body

Your arms react to your lower body moving toward the target.

and soft wrist joints, automatically flatten out and drop behind you.

The leading action of your lower body causes a quick separation. Basically, you're trying to leave your arms and hands (as well as the club) behind. Causing your club to trail is what positions it in the Slot.

It should feel as if the clubshaft and the clubhead are falling behind your body.

Your Right Elbow

As your arms drop and your lower body moves forward, your clubshaft should flatten. It shifts onto a lower plane (hopefully) without your even having to think about it. When I first instruct a student to drop down, however, he tends to pull hard with his left arm, a move that yanks the clubshaft in front of the body and destroys any chance of finding the Slot. The secret is to drop your right elbow close to your hip and underneath your right hand. Done correctly, it should feel as if your right elbow is moving toward the ball. This is one of the key moves that flattens the shaft. Try it a few times right now while you are sitting. Even without a golf club, you can imagine the shaft flattening out as you execute this important move.

If you need something to focus on as you transition from backswing to downswing, key in on your right elbow. From the top, it should feel as if your right elbow is trying to get inside your right pants pocket. I call this position the "Hitter's Pocket," with your right elbow in tight and the club behind your body. Once you're in the pocket, you're primed to deliver a powerful inside hit on the ball.

Note: It's important for you to understand that the force that reverses the swing's direction from back to forward comes first from the lower body and is relayed immediately to the upper body. The last thing to change direction is the clubhead.

Every good ball-striker sets the club into the Slot and gets his right elbow in close to his body. As long as your shaft flattens into this acceptable zone, your ball-striking will improve. From here, it's impossible to swing over the top.

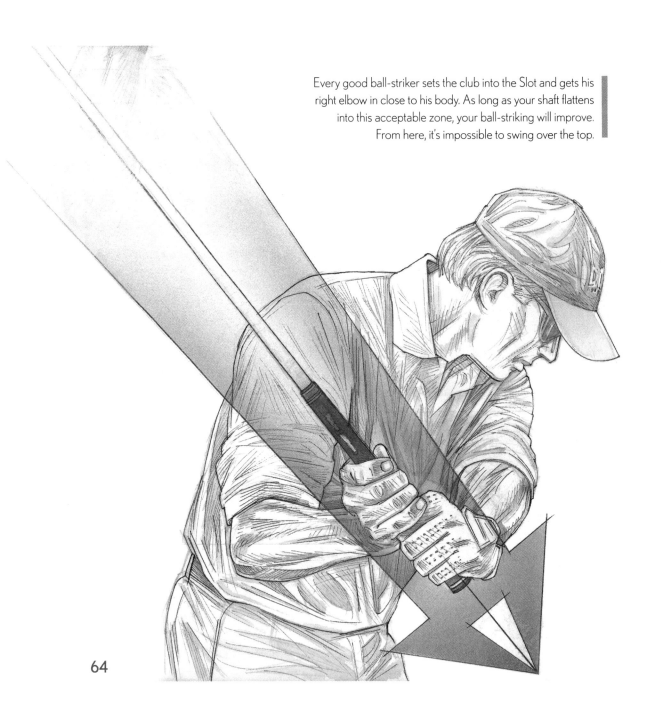

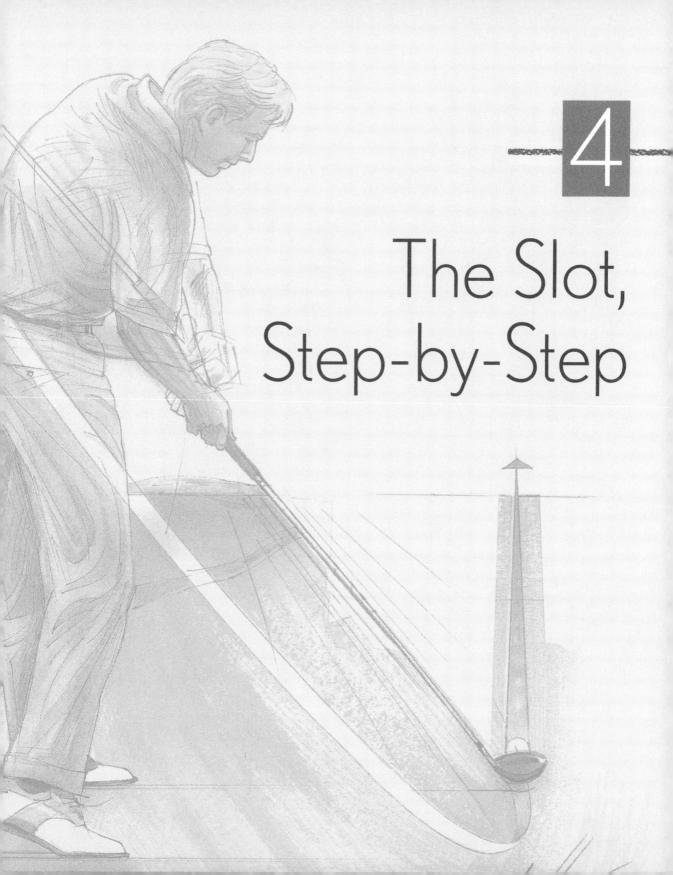

4

The Slot,
Step-by-Step

The Standard, or "Inside," Slot move is a fantastic way to improve clubface control because it eliminates rolling the clubface open in the backswing. It is also an excellent model to help you ingrain the feeling of looping the club to the inside at the start of the downswing, which allows you to achieve a better angle of attack. This is one reason that my staff and I teach this Slot Swing to most of the average amateur golfers who attend my golf schools. All three Slot Swings work, but we get great results from teaching the Inside Slot. The Inside Slot emphasizes a fundamental teaching idea in my school system, however, which is that the downswing arc is inside the backswing arc. And that's why it is so prominently featured in this chapter and throughout this book.

Although I've already discussed the key elements to finding the Slot, reviewing the swing step-by-step will give you a better idea of how these crucial moves fit into your overall motion. As you read through the following instructions, you'll confirm that I'm much less concerned with backswing positions than I am with downswing positions. (Don't get me wrong—the backswing is an important part of the overall Slot technique. Ben Hogan actually wrote about a "backswing slot" and how once he found it the quality of his ball-striking improved.) I do promote a simple and efficient backswing designed to help you find the Slot with ease and with greater consistency. As such, I set very few hard, fast rules for you to follow as you swing the club to the top. I've built this freedom into the Slot Swing because every single Tour player I've had the pleasure of working with or have analyzed, either in person or on tape, establishes different clubhead and clubshaft positions at the top of the backswing. The "perfect" backswing doesn't exist.

Slot Swing: Address

If your setup position is solid, you need to make only a few adjustments to set your swing on the right path toward finding the Slot. It's never a bad thing to work on your fundamentals, and it takes just a few minutes a day, in either your home or your office, to practice your address so that it becomes second nature when you're on the course.

- Your feet, knees, hips, shoulders, and eyes should be aligned approximately parallel, left of the target line.

- Your shoulders are relaxed and slightly hunched (not rigid or tensed). Your weight is balanced evenly between both feet.

- Your hips are pulled back, pants pockets behind your heels.

- Your arms are relaxed and hanging loose.

- The shaft angle matches the natural lie of the club.

- Your grip pressure = 5.

- Your hands are positioned between your pants zipper and the middle of your left thigh.

Take an Athletic Stance

Stand to the ball by bending slightly from your waist and moderately flexing your knees. Your knee flex is important—you should feel primed for action and ready to move in every possible direction, like a linebacker waiting for the snap. Although the Slot Swing doesn't require a ton of athleticism, there's no reason you shouldn't start it in an athletic stance. After all, you haven't moved anything yet.

Bend forward from your hips so that your tailbone is roughly four to eight inches outside your heels, and spread your feet to a comfortable width, making sure that both feet are firmly planted on the ground. You should feel the weight of your body flow down your legs, through your feet, and into the turf.

Strive for an athletic stance. You should feel like a linebacker ready to move in any direction.

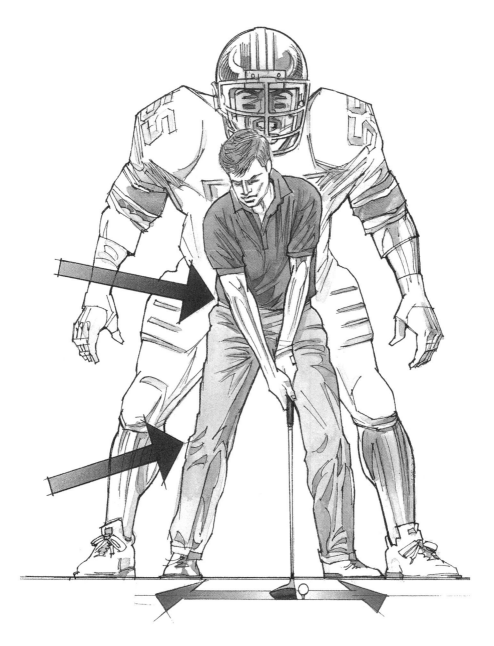

Set Your Hands

Many students ask me where they should position their hands. Since the ball position changes for each club in your bag, it makes sense for the hand position to change, too, right? Wrong. Ideally, the butt of whatever club you're swinging should point between your zipper and the crease in your left pant leg. Setting your hands too far in front of or behind the clubhead is not recommended.

Get Aligned

Most amateurs can nail the basic setup positions with only minimal practice but often struggle with aligning their bodies once they've settled into their stance. At first, I use the popular image of railroad tracks to make sure that the student's feet, shoulders, and hips are all pointing in the right direction. The railroad track image is widely used because it's virtually foolproof and simple and easy to check.

Imagine that your clubhead sits on and points down the outside rail of the railroad tracks. With that image, set your eyes, shoulders, hips, knees, forearms, and feet along the inside rail. Your shoulders are the most important; if they're not aligned, neither will be the items that they control (i.e., your arms, hands, and club).

Once you get the basics of setup alignment, adjustments can be made. Many top ball-strikers set up off the line, aiming left

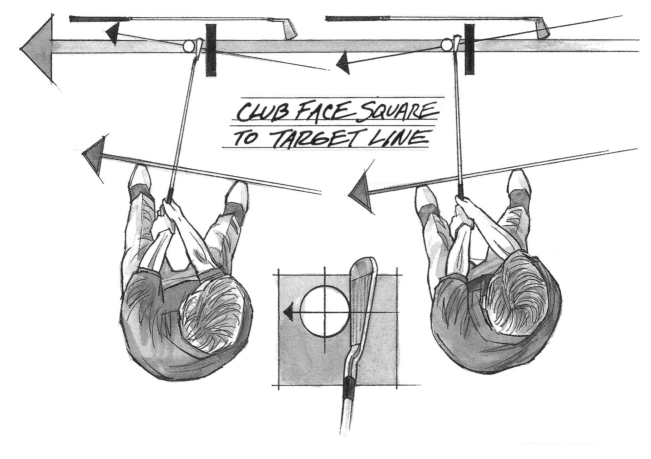

CLUB FACE SQUARE
TO TARGET LINE

Find the stance (open, closed, or neutral) that works best for you.

of the target, while others set up closed (right of the target). It's perfectly okay to adjust your stance to find the position that works best for you.

Get Comfortable

Make an effort to relax your shoulders. You've likely read other swing theories that instruct you to keep your shoulders back and your spine super straight. Ignore them. Following this advice invites tension into your swing. Be yourself. It's okay to slump your shoulders forward, keeping them loose. Jack Nicklaus did. Sam Snead did. So do Jim Furyk and many other great ball-strikers. When I see an amateur working hard to keep his back perfectly straight and his head extra high, I don't need to watch his swing. I already know it won't be good.

Tension is a killer. It has the incredible ability to undo all of your preparations and make swinging the club difficult to execute with balance and rhythm. If you get even the slightest sensation of tenseness or rigidity in your shoulders, back away, take a deep breath, and exhale very slowly. Do this a few times, and get back into your stance.

Keep the tension-free theme going and apply it to your arms and wrists. Shake them out before you take your stance. Watch Fred Couples the next time he's playing in a televised event. His arms look like wet noodles. It also helps if you keep your grip pressure at about a 5 or less on my scale of 1 to 10.

Light Grip #5

Favor a lighter grip pressure to keep tension
from creeping into your swing.

Standing too far from the ball is an invitation to swing the clubhead to the inside of the target line on your backswing and set in motion an over-the-top downswing. Stand closer to the ball, with only a fist's width separating your hands from your body. Standing taller to the ball like this makes it easier to start the club more outside so that it can loop to the inside at the top of your swing and find the Slot.

A move to focus on: Because one goal of the Inside Slot is to make sure you don't whip the club to the inside on your takeaway, stand closer to the ball (about two to three inches) so that you feel a little "taller" in your stance. This will force you to swing the club more to the outside at the start of your backswing. If you have trouble getting the clubhead out and up, stand extra close.

Slot Swing: Takeaway

Once you're settled into your address posture, it's time to hit the ignition. A good way to begin your swing is to pull the club back with your right hand. Keep your left arm soft. As you do this, notice how the club naturally swings more upward and more outside. A good checkpoint here is to make sure the clubhead remains outside your hands and in front of your chest. This helps guard against swinging the club too far to the inside.

Keep It Together

It's important that you start the club away from the ball using a "one-piece" action. By this, I mean moving the club, your arms, and your shoulders at the same time. If you do it

■ The clubhead moves above the target line.

■ Your weight begins rolling from your left foot to the right foot.

■ Your shoulders, arms, clubhead, and left knee move as one piece.

■ Your body remains relaxed and tension free.

■ Your forearms do not rotate, and the clubface does not rotate.

■ The clubhead stays outside your hands.

correctly, you'll almost immediately feel some pressure on the inside ball of your left foot, as if you're pushing off the ground. That's a good feeling, because it's evidence that you're already shifting your weight to your right side. (You'll get a better sense of weight shift with your longer clubs, especially your driver. Weight shift is very slight, if there's any at all, when you're swinging your short irons and wedges.)

As the club begins to move back, your head may move slightly away along with it. Allowing your head to "float" or rotate along with your swing actually encourages a stronger turn and a more efficient weight shift. Just make sure you keep your head movement to a minimum and both eyes on the ball.

Keep It Square

If you've been coming over the top for any period of time, you've likely fallen into the bad habit of rotating the clubface open in your takeaway. This goes hand in hand with swinging the club back to the inside, and it's bad news for your game.

Try to keep your forearms from rotating or your wrists from unduly turning. A good tip is to imagine that there's a flashlight in the center of your clubface. As you take the club back, try to keep the light shining on the ball. It'll feel as if the clubface is closed, but stick with it.

As you take the club back during your practice sessions, look down at your forearms and check to make sure that they're level with each other. If your right forearm looks lower than your left forearm, you've rotated your arms and set the club too far to the inside.

Keep your forearm rotation to a minimum.

Keep the clubface pointing at the ball deep into your takeaway. This is a good way to make sure that you don't whip the clubhead to the inside of the target line.

A move to focus on: The first move in your backswing is actually toward, not away from, your target. Most amateurs aren't aware of this microshift forward at the start of the swing, but it's a very real phenomenon.

Teaching legend Harvey Penick used the image of swinging a bucket of water to illustrate this move, what I like to call a "body press." If I asked you to swing the bucket without spilling any water, you'd naturally swing it forward prior to moving it back. If you simply jerked the bucket behind you, water would spill out.

I'm not sure how many buckets of water you've swung, but Penick's image makes its point: every swinging motion needs momentum. It's very difficult to make any sort of move from a dead stop, your backswing included. By first pressing slightly toward the target, you decrease the likelihood that you'll make a quick, jerky takeaway and increase your ability to swing with good tempo and rhythm.

It's a very simple move that'll pay big dividends in your motion. Here's one way to forward press: Settle into your stance, and once you're ready to begin your swing, push off your right instep and press your right knee and your hips toward the target. From this very small micromove forward, almost immediately begin your backswing.

Some players will use a slight hand press. That is, they push their hands slightly toward the target. This is okay, too. With a little practice, this ignition move will become second nature and almost undetectable, even by you. It will, however, definitely get you off to a smoother start in your swing and will reduce tension.

For Reverse Slot Swingers Only

From your address, immediately start turning your shoulders, hips, and arms. It should feel as if the clubhead is "sweeping" to the inside of the target line (picture it curving behind you on the ground). Keep your left arm close to your chest as you swing the club back.

Slot Swing: Halfway Back

One of the primary benefits of the inside loop Slot Swing is that it doesn't require you to make a big backswing turn or to coil hard against the resistance of your hips, something that most amateurs lack the flexibility and strength to accomplish. As I mentioned previously, the Slot places minimum emphasis on athleticism (yet it makes your swing very athletic).

 Your left knee is breaking in toward your right knee.

 Your hands are in front of your sternum.

 Your shoulders, arms, hands, and clubhead are still in "one piece."

 The clubhead is as far from the target as it will ever get.

Stay Outside

Your main priority here is to continue the upward path of the clubhead and fight off any urge to swing the club back to the inside of the target line. Ideally, the shaft should sit parallel to the ground and point directly down the target line at this point, but even here you have ample room for error. In an inside-loop swing, the clubshaft can be over or outside the plane. Most top ball-strikers don't hit the bull's-eye at this position. Simply focus on maintaining a relaxed feeling in your body.

Start Your Hinge

If I had made a dollar every time a student asked, "When should I hinge my wrists?" I'd be a rich man. It's a difficult question to answer. It's better to feel the answer yourself. Try the "Hands Back" drill.

Drill: Set up as you normally do, then smoothly swing your hands straight back, as if you're handing the club back to someone to your immediate right. If you keep your wrists soft and flexible, the clubhead will slightly lag behind your hands, but then your wrists will naturally hinge and the club will "catch up" and sit parallel to the ground by the time your hands reach waist height. This drill teaches you to allow your wrists to set the club effortlessly while maintaining the width of your swing, which is very important for power.

A move to focus on: A good checkpoint at the halfway-back position is to make sure that the clubshaft is in front of your chest. By this, I mean that your arms, hands, and club haven't rolled to the inside. To understand what this feels like, grip any iron by the steel just below the grip and stick the butt end in your stomach. Settle into a mock address position and swing the club back as you do in your takeaway, keeping the butt of the club in your stomach. Notice how the shaft remains in front of your chest. That's a good feeling at the start of your backswing.

You're solid at the halfway-back position if your arm swing matches up with the clubshaft. Notice how the right elbow naturally separates from the right side of the torso. If your right elbow sticks to your right side, you are jammed and you've swung the club too far to the inside (the swing plane is too flat).

Swing with the handle of your club in your stomach to learn the feeling of keeping the clubhead in front of your chest.

BUTT IN YOUR BELLY

SWING BACK & FORTH

For Reverse Slot Swingers Only

One thing to check is that your left arm and the club line up closely at the halfway-back position (even though the clubhead and the clubshaft are swinging under the plane). You can easily see this in a mirror or if you use a video camera. Although the club is well under your original shaft plane, your left arm is correspondingly inside, too. Your shaft position going up to the top should be flat—leaning closer to horizontal than vertical—and your right elbow should be sliding behind you.

Slot Swing: Three-Quarters Back

Now we've arrived at a more critical part of the backswing—the point where your hands have reached chest height in your backswing. In my early research with my colleague Carl Welty, it was this position that jump-started my interest in the Slot. At the three-quarters-back position, many good ball-strikers situate the shaft in a more upright position. Amateurs, on the other hand, often set the shaft much flatter. Once the shaft becomes flat at this point in the swing, the chances of an amateur approaching the ball from inside the target line on the downswing diminish dramatically (unless you employ the key moves of the Reverse Slot).

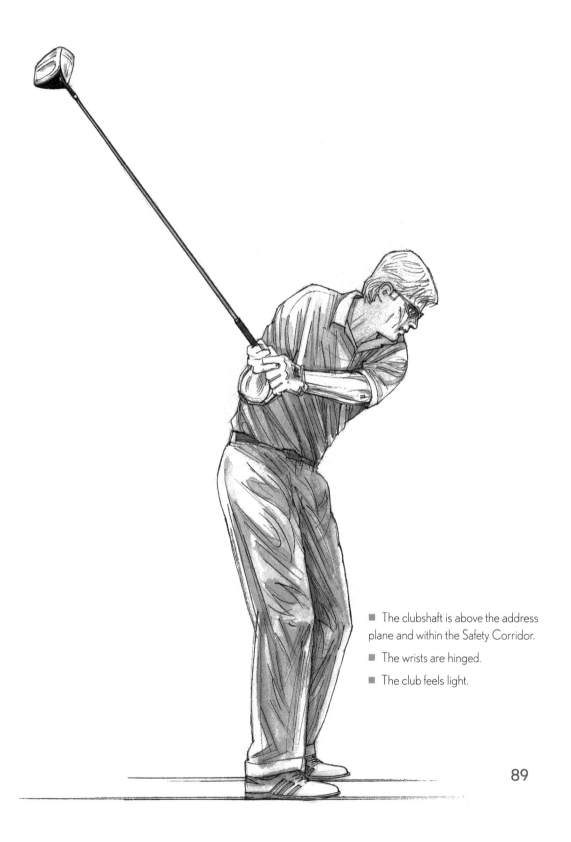

■ The clubshaft is above the address plane and within the Safety Corridor.

■ The wrists are hinged.

■ The club feels light.

Stay above the Address Plane

As you swing your hands to chest height, the shaft nearly bisects your upper right arm (from a down-target perspective). You don't have to be perfect here, as long as you keep the shaft above the plane it rested on at address and set it within the McLean Safety Corridor (see the illustration on page 93). The clubshaft will point well inside the target line and closer to your toe line. If the shaft ever falls below this plane (i.e., gets closer to being horizontal with the ground), you've strayed out of the acceptable shaft-position zone that is required for you to swing in the Slot.

The shaft is pointing skyward, and you should feel as if your thumbs are pointing up, not behind you.

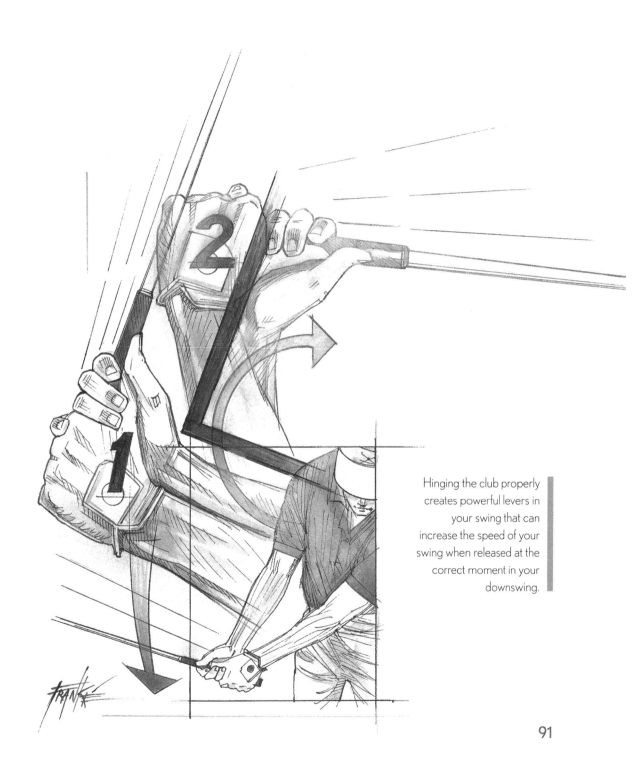

Hinging the club properly creates powerful levers in your swing that can increase the speed of your swing when released at the correct moment in your downswing.

91

Set Your L's (Short Irons Only)

At this point of your backswing, your wrist hinge is nearly complete. A result of a full (or nearly full) wrist hinge and the correct arm swing is the creation of three distinct L shapes: (1) between your left forearm and the clubshaft, (2) between your upper right arm and lower right arm, and (3) a tiny one between your right hand and right wrist. Not only are these L's important for keeping the shaft within the Safety Corridor, they function as highly charged power levers. When you release these levers through impact, they send volts of energy into your swing, exponentially increasing the speed of your clubhead.

If you hinge correctly and stay within the Corridor, the club will feel light in your hands (it feels heavy when you've swung too horizontally). This is a good thing—a lighter club is easier to swing fast.

A move to focus on: Before starting your swing, look down at your grip and count how many knuckles are visible on your left hand. Swing to your three-quarters-back position and stop. Count the knuckles again. If you see more knuckles, you rolled your left wrist and the shaft is too flat and out of the acceptable shaft-position zone. If you see fewer knuckles, you probably cupped your left wrist and the shaft is too upright (with the clubface wide open). Practice your backswing until you can count the same number of knuckles both at address and three-quarters back.

You only have to set the shaft within the Safety Corridor to guarantee a solid position at the top. There is no "perfect backswing."

Slot Swing: Top of the Backswing

The way you position your arms, your hands, and the shaft at the top of your swing is important. If you have a weak, narrow backswing, you'll have difficulty with power. If you have access to a full-length mirror, make your swing in front of it and stop at the top to check that the following positions are present in your swing.

Power Triangle

Looking down the target line, you should be able to draw a nice, tight triangle between your elbows and arms. Your elbows don't necessarily have to be level, as some instructors advocate. (If your right elbow is slightly higher than your left, then you've learned how this works.) This actually gives you more freedom to swing back down with more leverage and an extra dose of power, as Fred Couples, John Daly, J. B. Holmes, Jim Furyk, and Miller Barber do.

GOOD *Flow*

- Your left knee is braced but pointing behind the ball.

- Most of your weight is transferred to the right heel.

95

Steady Posture

It's important that you remain in a similar posture as the one you established at address. In other words, the angle your spine makes with the ground should be nearly the same at the top as it was at setup. Think about "staying in your framework." As you assess your posture, pay particular attention to your head. If it has moved dramatically up or down, it's a clear sign that you've lost your framework.

Hip Turn and Knee Break

Compare the position of your right hip and right knee at address to where they sit at the top of your backswing. It should look as if your right hip pocket has moved behind you, telling you that you correctly turned your hips on your backswing.

Try to move your right hip
behind to increase your coil.
Allowing your left knee to break
can increase your ability to turn.

RIGHT
POCKET

LEFT
POCKET

Clubshaft Pointing at the Target

If you look at the swings of better players, you'll notice that their arm swings and their shoulder turns stop at nearly the same time that they reach the end of their backswings.

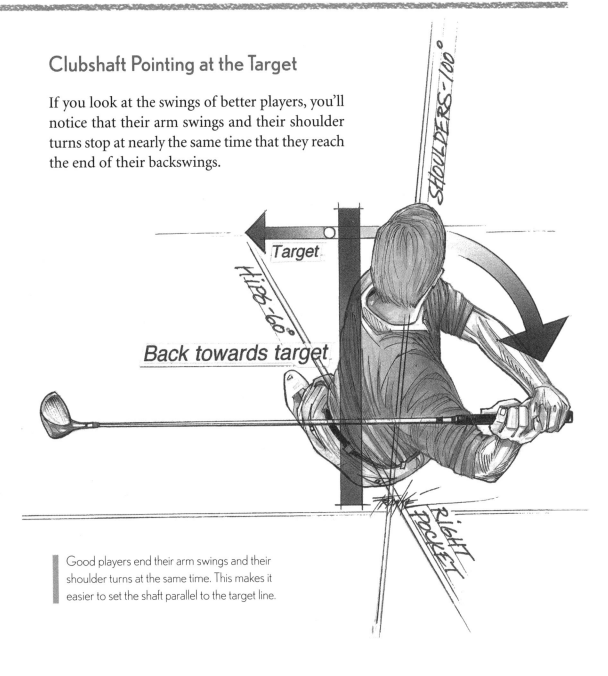

Good players end their arm swings and their shoulder turns at the same time. This makes it easier to set the shaft parallel to the target line.

If you're like most amateurs, you tend to stop your shoulders and then continue to swing the club back with your arms. This makes it more difficult to properly set the shaft at the top of the backswing and disrupts the timing of your swing.

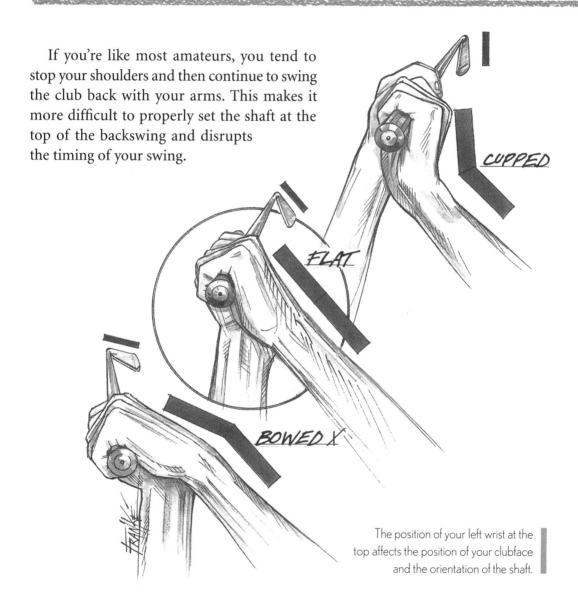

CUPPED

FLAT

BOWED X

The position of your left wrist at the top affects the position of your clubface and the orientation of the shaft.

If you're in an extremely across-the-line position, you've either lifted your right elbow too high into the air or dramatically cupped your left wrist. To counter this extreme position, try to keep your left wrist nearly flat and your elbows even as you reach the top of your backswing.

If you're extremely laid off, check the position of your hands. It's likely that you've swung them below your right shoulder. They should be even with or even slightly above the level of your right shoulder. That sets you up in a more vertical position and makes it easier to flatten the shaft on the way back down. It's impossible to hit good shots if you flatten the shaft on your downswing when the shaft is already too flat on your backswing.

Inside Slot Swing: Start of the Downswing

Once you've completed a solid backswing and set your body, you're ready to make the transition into the Slot. It's important that you feel comfortable before you make your first move down. Practice your top position, and make sure you're in good shape before you proceed. I promise that if you work on getting close to the positions outlined thus far, you'll be set in no time.

■ Your lower body is moving toward the target.

■ Your right foot is pushing into the ground.

■ Your right elbow is falling close to your right hip (the "Hitter's Pocket").

■ Your arms and hands are trailing the turning action of the lower body.

■ The clubshaft has shifted planes. Your knees are breaking toward the target.

Shift Your Knees toward the Target

The basic goal of your first move down is to change the plane of your swing and make your shaft position flatter than what it was going up. When you do it correctly, you'll feel the clubhead sink lower and drop behind you. It'll be a new sensation—when you swing over the top, the clubhead actually moves in front of you.

It's easy to look at the first move down and focus all of your attention on what your arms and hands are doing. I don't fault you for this. After all, your arms and hands establish drastically new positions in the Slot, and it looks as if they're controlling the action. In reality, this couldn't be further from the truth. Eventually, your hands and arms play a very passive role in slotting the club. They find the Slot in response to the movement of your lower body and the momentum it creates by shifting toward the target. As you first begin to master this fall-in action, however, you'll likely use your hands to achieve it. After all, the move will be very foreign to most amateurs and will take time to learn.

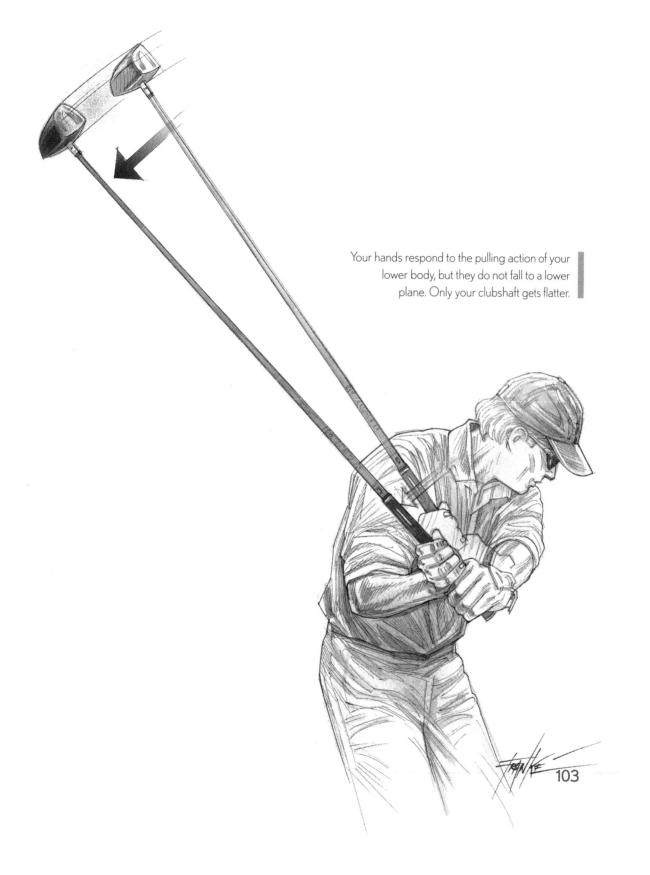

Your hands respond to the pulling action of your lower body, but they do not fall to a lower plane. Only your clubshaft gets flatter.

103

A move to focus on: Look again at the backswing photos on the previous pages. To amplify, you create three L shapes by the time you reach the three-quarters back position: (1) between your left forearm and the clubshaft, (2) between your upper right arm and lower right arm, and (3) a tiny one between your right hand and right wrist.

The secret to the Slot is to keep the L's intact deep into your downswing. Keeping the L's intact is another move that separates good ball-strikers from merely mediocre ones. To keep the L's together, you leave them alone. You do not pull down with your left arm. Instead, you shift your lower-body center. The force of this move may feel like a pull, and if you do it correctly, your right shoulder and right hip will drop.

Also, check the clubface. At the halfway-down position, it should be square (toe pointing up), no matter how you slot the club.

Reverse Slot swinger John Daly, like all Slot swingers, uses the force of his lower body to pull his arms into action, maintaining the L formed between the left forearm and the clubshaft deep into the downswing.

For Reverse Slot Swingers Only

As you loop your hands and arms outward to start your downswing (the moves that align your body correctly), it's crucial that you make the same forward lower-body shift that starts the Standard Slot downswing. This is a fundamental that can't be ignored. If you do it correctly, your shaft will "lie down" and fall behind your hands, even as your hands and arms loop outward. The shaft will not fly out in front of you as it does when you simply swing over the top.

A good way to feel the difference is to focus on your wrists. When you make the up-and-out move with your hands to slot the club at the start of your downswing, your left wrist will bow and your right wrist will cup. This is a much different wrist action from the one you use when you swing over the top. In a classic over-the-top slice swing, the left wrist cups and the right wrist bows. It's the same wrist action you'd use to cast a fishing line into a lake. That's why coming over the top is often called a "casting" move.

Slot Swing: Downswing, Impact, and Release

Once you find the Slot, most of the important work is done. But you can't stop there—you haven't even touched the ball yet.

Keep on Truckin'

Finding the Slot guarantees that the club will not get too steep or out in front of you on the way back to the ball. That in itself will solve most of your swing woes and will limit the frequency of your slices, pulls, and pull-slices. As you enter the impact zone in the Slot with your hands in position and with the clubface square, the only action required of you is to continue forward through the ball to a balanced finish, with 100 percent of your weight moving to your front foot. In fact, once you hit the Slot, you don't have to worry about manipulating the clubface at the bottom, something you feel that you have to do with an over-the-top swing so that you don't hit a slice or a pull. The centrifugal force, gravity, and an uninhibited free-swinging motion created by finding the Slot, combined with your body turn, will square the face automatically. This is why top players describe impact as a "no-hands feeling," even though they're releasing everything fully. What they're really describing is the feeling of no manipulation.

As you enter the impact zone in the Slot with your hands in position and with the clubface square, the only action required of you is to continue forward through the ball to a balanced finish, with 100 percent of your weight moving to your front foot.

Play Ball

Because the club is starting to move very fast at this point in your swing, it's difficult to talk about positions. Over the years, I've found it helpful to relate the downswing and the impact to something with which the student is more familiar. For most people, that's swinging a baseball bat. Most of us have done it, and we did a fairly good job without even thinking about it (at least, not as much as we think about our golf swings). What I like about the baseball comparison are the similarities between swinging a bat and swinging a golf club through impact and into the release and their reliance on finding the Slot.

In both swings, the "stick" flattens (or lowers) at the start of the forward-swing. In baseball, the batter actually strides toward the pitcher, meaning that his first move in hitting is a forward step. Then he flattens the angle of the bat to nearly horizontal. It's a significant move, but not even a Little Leaguer thinks about it. It just happens. As the bat flattens out onto its new plane, the batter is rotating his hips like mad, while he drops his right elbow down and forward. Sound familiar?

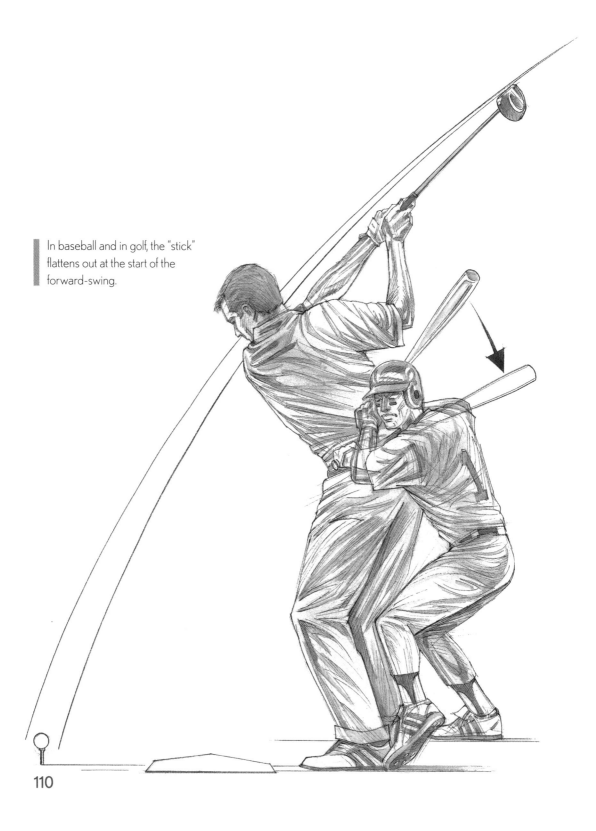

In baseball and in golf, the "stick" flattens out at the start of the forward-swing.

110

By the time the ball is halfway to the plate, a baseball player has already slotted the club by shifting his weight forward, dropping his hands, and flattening out his swing plane. He's rotating his hips and straightening his front leg, but he still holds the bat back so that he can delay his decision to swing for as long as possible and get a better read on the pitch.

As you swing into impact, begin releasing the angles in your elbows and wrists, just as a homerun hitter does in baseball.

Now comes the hit. In both sports, the act of contact is simply a matter of continuing your body turn and releasing each of your power levers: the three L's created in your back-swing. Your wrists unhinge and your right elbow straightens through impact. If your timing

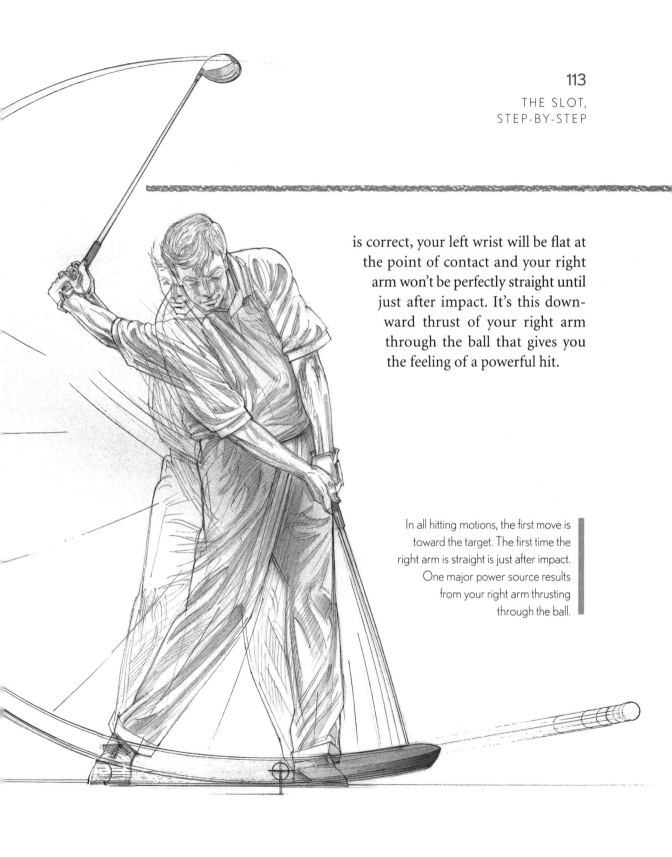

is correct, your left wrist will be flat at the point of contact and your right arm won't be perfectly straight until just after impact. It's this down- ward thrust of your right arm through the ball that gives you the feeling of a powerful hit.

In all hitting motions, the first move is toward the target. The first time the right arm is straight is just after impact. One major power source results from your right arm thrusting through the ball.

If you watch baseball, you'll notice that each of the game's best homerun hitters lets go of the bat with his right hand after impact. Mark McGuire did this, and so does Albert Pujols. Study Vijay Singh, Fred Couples, and Phil Mickelson, and you'll see them make a similar move. None of these players completely lets go with his top hand, but it does come off the club. The reason for this, I believe, is because they release the clubs (or the bat, in Pujols's case) so hard. As a big hitter releases his right forearm and right wrist, the right wrist bows and turns on top of the left hand. As this bow takes shape, the left wrist cups, whipping the clubhead out toward the target and almost pulling the arms straight out of their sockets.

It's unlikely that you'll generate enough speed to pull your right hand off the club, as Vijay does, but it's important that you see how the right wrist bows downward after impact. The club should feel like an extension of your right arm in your release. I produced a DVD called *The Powerline* entirely on this very subject, which very few golfers know or understand.

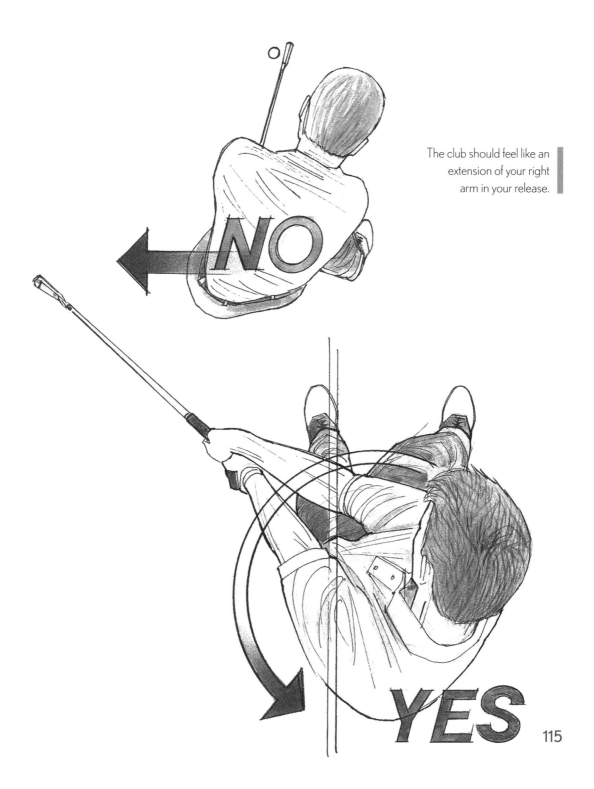

The club should feel like an extension of your right arm in your release.

NO

YES

Slot Swing: Finish

After you release the club, the momentum of your swing should pull you into a nice, balanced finish position. Because all of the motion of the swing is over, the finish is a fairly easy aspect of your swing to evaluate.

- Your right shoulder is closer to the target than your left shoulder is.

- Your grip pressure is light.

- The clubshaft crosses through the back of your head, not drooping over your shoulder like a laundry bag.

- Nearly all of your weight is over your left leg.

- Your hips are facing the target or left of the target, and your shoulders are turned more than your hips.

- Complete balance—you should be able to hold your finish without tipping or leaning. Picture your right heel up, like a quarterback throwing deep downfield.

117

As you practice the moves discussed in this chapter, your swing should begin to feel more athletic. You should sense that your swing is beginning to flow with rhythm and balance as you apply the "shift-rotate-throw" action sequence that is seen in all other athletic hitting motions. An athletic swing motion has the best chance of being repeated and of working under pressure. A contrived and effort-filled "perfect" swing will break down much faster under competition.

Human beings have used the principles of an athletic sequence since the dawn of time. When early cavemen went out to hunt, the tribe sent its most skilled hunters—the ones who could throw spears the best. These individuals applied the same Slot ideas presented in this book and based their throwing action on a sequence of moves. The caveman hunter cocked the spear back wide and returned it in a narrow forward move before letting it fly. He moved the spear on two planes, with the forward plane lying inside the back plane. The tribe couldn't afford to send out a hunter who didn't know how to perform the correct throwing action to bag that night's dinner. An Inside Slot action was the difference between life and death. Luckily for you, this is only golf.

5

Putting It All Together

W e've covered a few positions thus far, and each one is an essential piece to the Slot puzzle, which will ensure that you create a flatter shaft angle on your downswing so that you can't come over the top.

This chapter focuses on some of your larger muscles and body parts and how to move them so that the positions inherent in the Slot Swing take shape as if by magic. If the positions described in chapter 4 make up the engine of the Slot Swing, the following moves are the gasoline. Performed correctly, they make slotting the club second nature.

Overall Body Action

Ben Hogan wrote in his *Five Lessons*, "The body swings the arms." He also wrote, "The action of the arms is motivated by the movements of the body." Among other ideas, these words provide extremely valuable clues to the secrets of the Slot Swing.

After all of my study and research using high-speed cameras and videotape on an almost daily basis, one of the biggest differences I see between the recreational and the accomplished player is the way they begin the forward move toward the ball (i.e., the first move down from the top of the backswing). Typically, a professional is patient and uses the proper sequence of moves to take him into and through impact. If you're like most of the amateurs I teach, however, you impatiently hit from the top, either with your hands and arms or by spinning your shoulders. Starting the downswing like this gives you little chance to deliver the clubhead into the ball with power and consistency.

Ben Hogan epitomized the proper sequencing of downswing events: shifting (of the lower body), rotating (the core), dropping (the arms, the hands, and the clubhead), keeping the shoulders back for as long as possible, and, finally, throwing (extending the right arm through the ball).

123

In all athletic throwing or hitting actions, the golf swing included, the lower body makes the first move forward and does it in such a way that there's no specific moment at which the backswing ends and the forward swing begins. If you ever get the chance to see a pro's swing on videotape, move it frame by frame at the top and you'll see that the club is still going back as the lower body begins to move forward. I point this out simply as fact, but I normally recommend that you don't think about it when you play. This two-way motion concept is for the range only and not for the course.

The important thing is that once you load pressure inside the right leg as you complete your shoulder coil, you're now poised to go the other way. Start your shift forward with your lower body acting as the leader. Follow these steps:

1. The first move to initiate the downswing is to shift your weight onto your front foot. First, bump your hips right of the target. (Your hips will begin to turn after this initial lateral bump. Keep in mind that as all of this takes place, the clubhead is still going back.)

2. Once you start your shift, keep your shoulders back.

3. Lower your arms and flatten the shaft.

4. As your club enters the delivery zone, with your weight firmly over your left leg, release your entire right side through the ball.

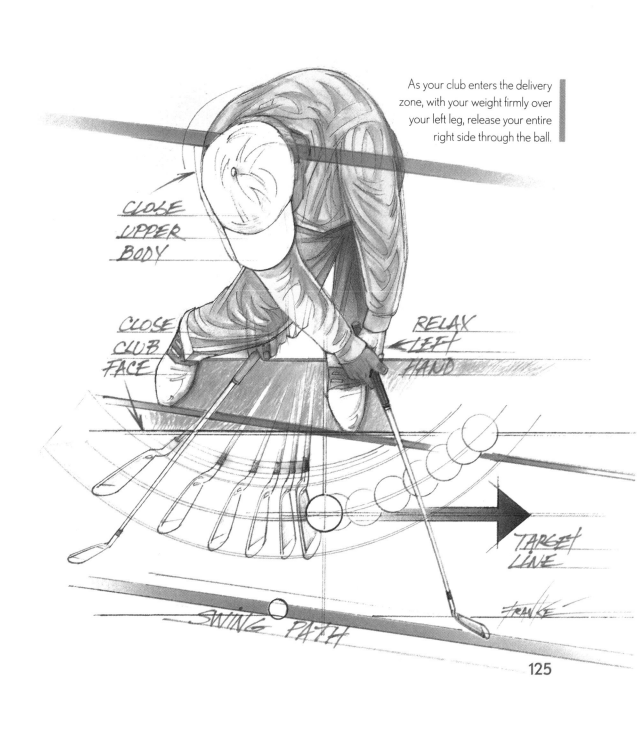

As your club enters the delivery zone, with your weight firmly over your left leg, release your entire right side through the ball.

CLOSE UPPER BODY

CLOSE CLUB FACE

RELAX LEFT HAND

TARGET LINE

SWING PATH

FRANKE

125

To simplify, making a fundamentally solid downswing is *shifting*, *rotating*, *dropping*, and *throwing*. When you hear me mention the correct sequence of downswing moves, these are the items I'm talking about. They are the same moves you would make to throw a rock in a somewhat sidearm motion to skip across a lake.

It's important to realize that while your lower body shifts and your torso turns, the shaft responds to their movement by falling on plane into the Slot.

Moving Center

Whenever I mention that the lower body initiates the forward shift toward the ball from the top of the backswing, a student invariably asks, "How much does the lower body shift?" Good question.

When I look at the swings of Tour professionals and better amateurs, I can see the centers of their lower bodies (I'll focus on their belt buckles) move as much as six inches forward of their original address positions to impact. That's a fairly significant shift and certainly proves that there's a strong lateral component to high-level swings. The left hip will come close to lining up over the left knee. The left knee will get right on top of the left foot.

On this topic, I always recall a conversation I had with Roberto de Vincenzo. I used to watch Roberto and Sam Snead play the Senior Circuit in Orlando during the mid-1970s. Roberto told me that when he was really hitting the ball well, he felt like he was hitting it with his stomach. What I believe he felt was the force of his lower-body center and the thrust it generated by moving forward in time with the turning action of his upper body.

Roberto's stomach-swing concept might be a bit esoteric, but now that you know a little more about the importance of your lower-body center, it's a brilliant swing concept to borrow from. It's a move that really helps put the golf club into the Slot.

Note: Although it's important to think about your lower-body center and shifting it forward during your downswing, by all means don't forget about your upper-body center (indicated by your sternum). It moves forward, too, although not as much as the lower center. When you strike the ball with an iron, your upper-body center should be about an inch forward of the space it occupied at address.

That being said, most amateurs have the bad habit of moving their upper-body centers too far in front of their original positions. This happens when you spin your shoulders hard from the top, instead of shifting your lower body forward and dropping the shaft into the Slot. Good players suffer from the opposite problem. They tend to hang too far back and actually move their upper-body centers away from the target, creating extra spine tilt. When this happens, the swing path becomes very inside-out and very shallow.

Right-Arm Action

One thing that many top PGA Tour professionals agree on is that the action of the right arm is crucial to generating power in the swing. As I've mentioned previously, this action is very similar to the one you'd use to skim a stone across the surface of a pond or throw a ball. Focusing your attention on your right arm and right side will help you improve much faster

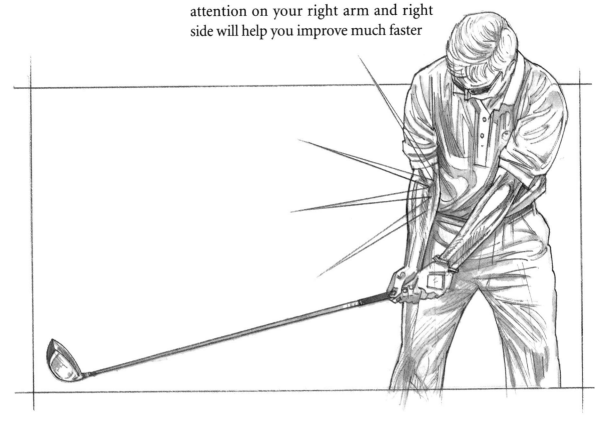

than trying to train your much-less-coordinated left side (if you're naturally right-handed) will.

The great champion and hall-of-famer Byron Nelson (they named the perfect-swing robot "Iron Byron" after him) always called the right arm a "floater." By that, he meant that the right arm swings freely during the takeaway. I really like this concept. The last thing you want is to attach your right arm to your right side early in your backswing. Rather, let it "float" away from your body so that your right elbow comes off your right side. Doing this helps create width and leverage and turns your right arm into your swing's whip. If you tuck your right arm close to your body early in the backswing, you'll narrow your swing arc and weaken the turn of your upper torso. In short, you'll lose leverage and the ability to use the right arm as a whip—and you'll lose power.

Your right arm floats away from your right side during your takeaway and then reattaches on the way back down, mostly due to the pulling action of your lower-body shift.

As important as the right-arm movement is on the backswing, it's the move from the top of the backswing to the beginning of the downswing that separates top ball-strikers from average players. Basically, your right arm falls in and reattaches itself to your right side as your lower body shifts toward the target at the start of the downswing. Going from this floating right-arm position to one where your right elbow almost feels glued to your side is crucial to slotting the club consistently.

Knee Action

Your knees are very easy to take for granted, but they're an important component of creating power and finding the Slot.

As you start your backswing, "break" your left knee inward and behind the ball. At the completion of your backswing, an imaginary line drawn across your kneecaps should point at least 25 degrees to the right of your target line.

This subtle break has powerful repercussions. It automatically frees up your hips so that they can turn more easily, and it increases your ability to transfer your weight properly to your right side. Try turning your hips while keeping both knees braced; then try it again while kicking in your left knee. Amazing, huh?

As you start your backswing, "break" your left knee inward and behind the golf ball.

131

You'll notice that as you break your left knee and turn your hips while bringing the club to the top, your knees rotate as well. The key to stopping your hips from overturning is to retain the flex in your right knee. Of course, every turn that happens going back must reverse itself going forward. But before you rotate your knees to the left on your way back down to the ball, shift them laterally toward the target (à la Lee Trevino and the move we discussed in chapter 3). Once your knees start to shuttle back to the target, they'll unwind along with your hips. At impact, a line drawn across your knees should point 30 to 40 degrees to the left of the target line.

The X-Factor

When most golfers think of a turn or a coil, the majority think about their shoulders. In reality, however, the most important element of your coil is your hips. In much the same way, your left-knee break frees up your hip turn, and your hip turn frees up your shoulders, allowing you to rotate them farther behind the ball and ramp up the potential energy of your swing.

Note: One cornerstone of my teaching is that the lower body should resist the turning action of the upper body. But resistance can be overdone, and most amateurs don't have the flexibility to coil their upper bodies tightly against their lower bodies. I recommend that you turn your hips between 40 and 60 degrees in your backswing.

The more you turn your shoulders, the more likely it is that you'll create a bigger difference between the amount of shoulder turn and the amount of hip turn. This is how you produce torque and is the basis of my X-Factor theory.

Your shoulders make the biggest turn of all during your backswing, and they do so on their very own axis. They don't turn on a level plane, like a merry-go-round (which would bring your arms and club too far to the inside and around). Conversely, they don't tilt forward and turn like a Ferris wheel (which would make your swing too steep). The correct way to turn your shoulders during your backswing and to maximize your X-Factor is to feel as if your right shoulder is going up and behind your head as your left shoulder travels level and behind the ball. This is a feeling I have taught that usually works wonders. Your shoulders actually turn on a 90-degree axis to your spine, however, meaning that your left shoulder absolutely goes down during your backswing. So, in some cases, I also teach "left shoulder down." Monitor your shoulder rotation with a video camera to see which feeling works best for you.

The X-Factor directly relates to the Slot Swing because the creation of torque acts like a wound spring. Because the hips

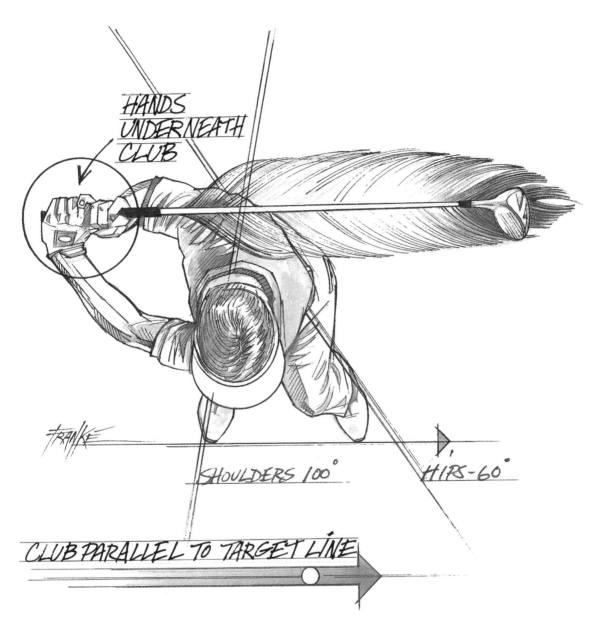

HANDS UNDERNEATH CLUB

SHOULDERS 100°

HIPS-60°

CLUB PARALLEL TO TARGET LINE

FRANKE

134

The stronger your X-Factor (the difference between your shoulder turn and hip turn), in general the stronger your power potential.

and the legs resist in the backswing, they move easily to lead the clubshaft. When the lower leads, the clubshaft responds by lowering and flattening on plane.

The Y-Factor

The Y-Factor is, for the most part, your X-Factor from a face-on view. I developed the Y-Factor analysis after studying videotapes of top players from around the world. In watching these high-level swings with a driver, I noticed that the left shoulder always moves behind the ball during the backswing. It's one of the fundamental elements of power.

The Y-Factor starts with an imaginary straight line that extends upward from the front edge of the left hip. At the end of the backswing, most good players have moved their left shoulders a solid fifteen inches or more behind this line. Lines connecting the backswing shoulder position, the address shoulder position, and the point indicated by the front edge of the left hip form a "Y."

Analyzing your Y-Factor on video is a unique way to see how much you're moving and loading during your back-swing. A good way to think about improving your Y-Factor or making a larger shoulder turn (because most amateurs don't turn back enough) is to turn your left shoulder into the spot

YES

NO

Turning your left shoulder correctly away from the ball sets you powerfully behind the ball with most of your weight over your right foot. This allows you to make the lateral shift toward the target that pulls your arms and hands down and slots the club correctly.

that your right shoulder held at address. Or try to get your left shoulder directly over the inside of your right heel.

When you draw the line straight down from the left hip, you should also see your left hip move a few inches away from that line when you hit a long iron or a driver.

The stronger your Y-Factor, the better your positions will be at the top of your backswing. If you coil strong and then start down with the proper motion, your golf club will have a much better chance of working on "automatic pilot" and finding the Slot with ease.

Tempo

Without a doubt, there's a timing element to the Slot, and if you're used to making rushed, hurried swings from the top, you might have some difficulty with the moves discussed thus far. All amateurs can benefit from better tempo. I like my students to count out a tempo in their heads. Several great teachers of the past have employed the "one-and-two" count. I think it's a good one to use. As you start your backswing, count out a slow "one," say "and" at the top, and then swing down on the "two." This tempo trick really works. It gives you just the right amount of time to loop the clubhead at the top and lower the shaft.

Weight Transfer

The weight you feel in your feet and legs needs to move from an even distribution at address to one that favors your right foot and the inside of the right thigh at the top of your backswing. The extent of this weight transfer depends on the golf club you're hitting: short irons require less weight transfer and longer clubs, especially your driver, require more. (The lie of the ball and the type of shot you want to hit also affect weight-distribution changes, but that's for another time.) If you're looking for a hard average percentage to follow, I suggest transferring 75 percent of your weight to your right leg during your backswing. For example, if you weigh 200 pounds, then 50 pounds should be on your left foot and 150 pounds should be on your right foot when you reach the top of your backswing. When you watch a good golfer swing, check his feet; if you see his feet move, then you know his weight is moving.

At the top of your backswing, most of your weight should be on your right foot. Your weight shifts forward from your backswing so that most of it sits on your left foot at impact.

BACKSWING

ADDRESS

FINISH

140

Head Movement

Yes, your head moves during your swing. Actually, it can move, turn, or do a combination of the two. A nice way to think about head movement is that your chin makes its own little swing, rotating back and through. I suggest that you avoid trying to keep it dead still, as some instructors would like you to do. Restricting head movement is the fastest way to disrupt your move away from the ball, negating your weight shift, X-Factor, and Y-Factor. This restriction can have horrible effects on your downswing as well, which in turn will reduce your ability to hit the Slot consistently. It can also lead to back and neck problems.

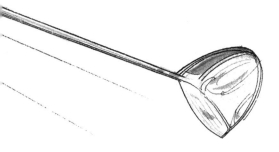

Allowing your head to rotate during your swing improves your weight shift, X-Factor, and Y-Factor.

Club Balance

Take a good look at your driver or one of your irons. To many average players, it's a strange-looking implement, but if you can think back to your college physics class, you'll recognize it in its simplest form: a weight attached to the end of a fulcrum. As with any weight/fulcrum arrangement, the weight gets heavier and becomes difficult to move when it falls off balance. This happens when you make the mistake of rolling the shaft into an extremely flat position during your downswing (the precursor to the over-the-top downswing). Once the club gets heavy, it tends to negatively influence your body's action and make your swing plane even flatter as you reach the top. You end up in a severely laid-off position (the shaft pointing way left of the target line), with absolutely zero chance of hitting the Slot.

On the other hand, when the weight and the fulcrum are in harmony, the weight actually feels lighter. This happens when you make the shaft more vertical in your backswing. It's a real feeling, and you'll sense it the first time you execute the backswing moves we discussed in chapter 4.

If your clubhead feels heavy no matter what position you try, experiment with slowing down your body's pivot. When you pivot too early (a move that logically seems like a good one to make), the clubhead may possibly get stuck too far behind you, and the shaft becomes flat and off balance.

Light

HEAVY

A good checkpoint in your back-swing is to sense whether the club feels heavy or light. If you swing your club too flat during your backswing, it will fall off balance and feel "heavy."

143

Length of the Swing

Watch any Tour event on TV and you'll see many players with long backswings, while others have very short backswings. Obviously, the ability to strike the ball with power and with the center of the clubface does not necessarily depend on how far you take the club back. What's not so obvious is that every pro has spent years fine-tuning his downswing and adjusting his first move forward to match up with the length of his backswing. If you make a mismatch, you'll have difficulty finding the Slot.

If you like to make a long, fluid backswing...

Increase the amount of lateral motion toward the target as you start back down. Increasing your lateral motion here gives the clubhead more time to "catch up" with your swing and fall into the Slot. If you don't increase the amount of lateral shift, your clubhead will tend to get stuck too far behind your body and you'll miss the Slot.

If you like to make a short, compact backswing...

Rotate your hips and torso faster on your downswing. This encourages the club to loop from its short position and fall into the Slot.

6

How to Groove the Slot Swing

I t's one thing to read swing instructions, but putting them to good use is an entirely different story. Taking the written word to the course doesn't happen overnight—every player has to pay his dues on the range, and even this isn't enough. If you hit a thousand balls a week, you won't make any improvements in your swing or increase your ability to hit the Slot consistently if you're not repeating the correct motions. That's the danger of unsupervised practice.

Since it's impossible for me to watch you practice the necessary moves at your local range or practice area, you can use the following drills to cultivate the correct form. Drills are the conduit between instruction and implementation. A carefully constructed drill ensures that you're not wasting your practice time grooving bad technique or simply hitting balls without having concrete objectives and goals.

Each of the following drills tackles specific areas within the Slot Swing. Don't try to do them all at the same time; get one down pat before moving on to the next, then revisit the drill or drills that help your swing. You'll find that your practice time can actually become serious learning time, and that practice, indeed, can be fun. A major success component of my golf schools is the training our instructors go through, which enables them to build an improvement plane for each student. I know that if you develop your practice habits and follow an appropriate swing drill, improvement is guaranteed. Remember, you can perform many drills away from the range.

Drill #1: Rock Toss

How to Do It

Grab a golf ball in your right hand, stand at ease, and swing your right arm back. Now try to throw the ball as if you're skipping a stone off a lake. Since you didn't establish an athletic base to begin your throw, you may have to think twice about how to get your right arm in action and sling it in a somewhat sidearm move so that the ball will skip. The correct way to do it is to start your lower body moving forward and pull your right elbow into your right side. If you make these moves fast enough, your right wrist will bend back and you'll feel your right forearm actually move back at the same time that your right elbow moves forward. Once this happens, release your right forearm past your body by straightening your right elbow. The ball will come out with more force than you ever thought possible.

The action of skipping a stone off the lake is the same motion your right arm makes in the Slot downswing. Keep the hand on top of the ball going back, then under going forward.

What It Does

This simple drill grooves the correct right arm action for the Slot Swing. Your first move down from the top is a lateral shift of your lower body toward the target. Your right elbow then moves down plane, flattening the shaft and bringing the club into the proper delivery position. The Rock Toss Drill captures each of these moves beautifully.

Drill #2: Waist-High Hits

How to Do It

Using your 6-, 7-, or 8-iron, make small swings, stopping your hands at waist height in your backswing and waist height in your through-swing. Abbreviated swings like this are excellent tools. Suddenly, you're not concerned with how far you hit the ball. These swings are also good for slowing down your motion so that you can concentrate on specific parts and make sure you're doing all of the little things right.

As you swing your arms back to waist height in your backswing, hinge your wrists so that the clubshaft sits nearly perpendicular to the ground (the vertical shaft position I recommend in the Standard Slot Swing). Now, start your downswing by consciously dropping the clubhead behind you and changing the shaft position from vertical to more horizontal.

(It won't get to horizontal, but it's a good idea to exaggerate the way it feels when you try to learn a new technique.) Be careful to flatten the shaft, not your arms. It might be very useful to visualize the Jim Furyk loop when you try this drill.

What It Does

This drill helps you groove the important loop move at the start of your downswing that makes your downswing plane flatter than your backswing plane. It's a good idea to have a friend stand behind you and check that you're correctly flattening out the shaft.

Drill #3: Closed-Stance Swings

How to Do It

Set up to the ball with any club and picture a clock on the ground, with the ball in the middle of the face and the 12 pointing toward the target. Make your Slot Swing, but this time focus on swinging the clubhead over the 7 as you approach the ball and over the 1 after contact. If this is difficult for you, address the ball with a slightly closed stance (right foot pulled back from the target line). Now hit the inside quadrant of the golf ball.

Practicing from a closed stance and visualizing an inside approach trains you to trace an inside path to the ball.

What It Does

This drill teaches you to approach the ball from inside the target line—a mainstay of the Slot Swing. You are almost forced to loop the club to the inside attack track. It's the only way to hit the ball way out to the right of your stance line.

Drill #4: Fade Stance Swings

How to Do It

This is one of my favorite drills for midrange to advanced golfers because it fixes a steep, over-the-top swing (i.e., the most damaging swing you can make). Tee up your driver, pick out a target on the range, and then set up a good twenty yards or more left of it. Although you're aimed way left, try to hit the ball straight at your target.

Even if you're new to the game, you'll instinctively begin to make all the right moves necessary to push the ball off to the right. Specifically, you'll shorten your right side coming down (as your right shoulder and right hip are pinching together), and you'll drop your right elbow into your right side.

This is one drill I used very successfully with PGA Tour player Peter Jacobsen when he was getting too steep with his swing.

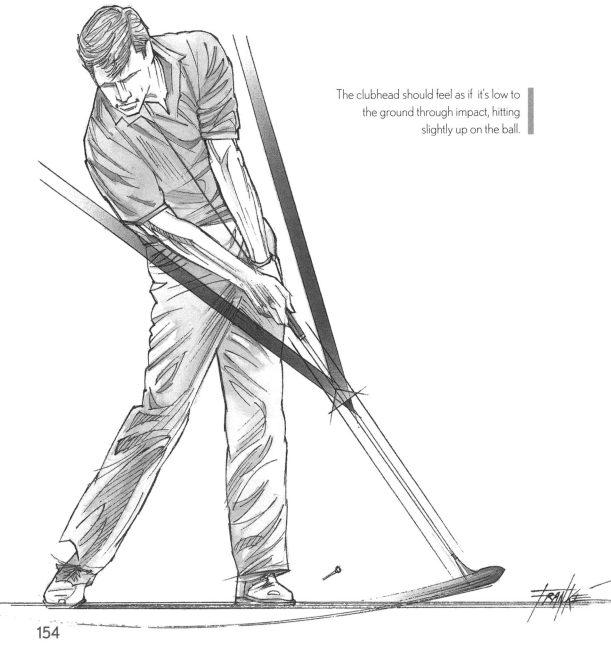

The clubhead should feel as if it's low to the ground through impact, hitting slightly up on the ball.

154

What It Does

This drill helps you get a sense of what an inside-out swing feels like and trains your right side to move down, under, and then forward during your downswing. These are crucial elements of the Slot and are also polar opposites of the moves you typically make when you swing over the top and across the ball.

Drill #5: Wall Swings

How to Do It

Find a high wall and stand two feet in front of it. Address an imaginary ball with your back facing the wall, and swing the club back. Your goal in this part of the drill is to move the shaft all the way to the top without brushing your clubhead against the wall.

Once you've reached the top without touching the wall, start your swing back down. As I discussed, start your downswing by shifting and turning your lower body and letting your arms respond to its movement. If you do it correctly, the clubhead should fall against the wall (i.e., find the Slot). Keep the clubhead sliding down the wall for several inches.

Perform this drill slowly. At first, the clubhead and the shaft will feel as if they're too far behind your body when the clubhead touches the wall on your downswing. That's the feeling you're after. If you have difficulty getting the clubhead to touch, make sure you're keeping your left arm in tight against your chest. When you keep your left arm in tight as you drop your arms in response to the shifting and turning action of your lower body, the clubshaft will flatten and the clubhead will hit the wall.

Continue your downswing in slow motion. Check that the clubhead maintains contact with the wall for the first twelve to eighteen inches of your downswing.

What It Does

This drill teaches you how to drop your hands to the inside and switch the clubshaft onto a lower plane. This is the essence of the Slot.

Drill #6: Figure Eight

How to Do It

Address the ball with any club. As you look down, picture an imaginary figure eight on the ground, with the top of the eight pointing at the target. (If you can paint the figure eight on the grass, even better. Just check with your superintendent. You can also draw the eight with chalk in your garage or driveway.)

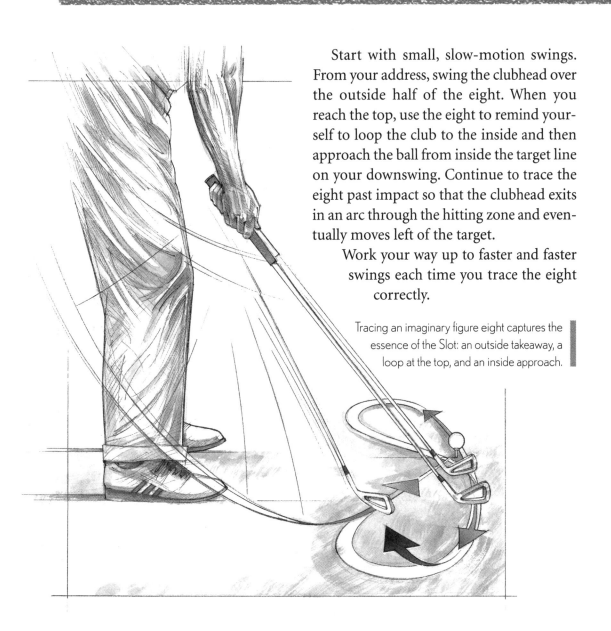

Start with small, slow-motion swings. From your address, swing the clubhead over the outside half of the eight. When you reach the top, use the eight to remind yourself to loop the club to the inside and then approach the ball from inside the target line on your downswing. Continue to trace the eight past impact so that the clubhead exits in an arc through the hitting zone and eventually moves left of the target.

Work your way up to faster and faster swings each time you trace the eight correctly.

Tracing an imaginary figure eight captures the essence of the Slot: an outside takeaway, a loop at the top, and an inside approach.

What It Does

The figure eight is a road map to hitting the Slot. Tracing it with your clubhead provides you with a real sense of how to swing straighter back and then inside. It will train a loop of the club at the top of your backswing.

As do all of my students, you'll discover that finding the Slot more often makes a concrete and very real improvement in the quality of your ball-striking, and, hopefully, that it really isn't that daunting of a task. Inherent in the Slot Swing is a wide margin for error in your backswing. It forgives—you don't have to follow a regimented path on the way up. As I've repeated, however, you do need to find the correct Slot on the downswing, and as you practice the Slot technique and apply the drills presented in this chapter, realize that old habits might die hard. If you've been swinging over the top by maneuvering the clubshaft into a steep plane and then cutting across the ball on your downswing, the changes won't happen overnight. Taking the club away more upward and to the outside will be a completely different sensation, but realize that this new backswing motion leaves you with a ton of room to swing inside on the downswing (the Furyk, Trevino model).

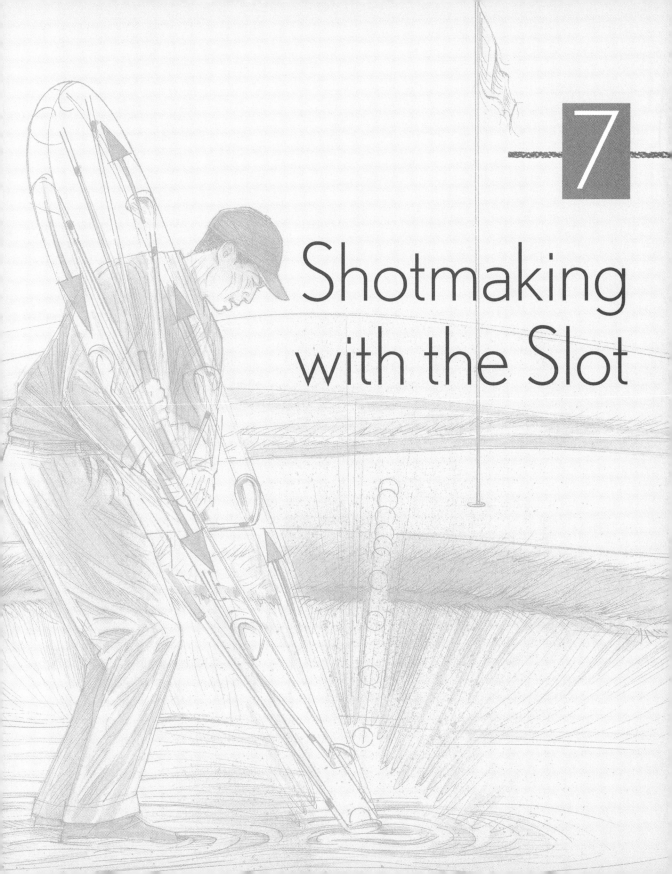

7

Shotmaking with the Slot

U p until now, you've likely assumed that hitting the Slot applies only to full swings with your driver and irons. True—the Slot is the fundamental key to generating powerful contact consistently and with minimal effort. But think back to your last round. Sure, you made a lot of full swings off the tee and from the fairway, but you also hit a lot of pitches and chips and even found the sand a few times. And if you think back, you can likely recall a situation where you hit through the fairway on a dogleg because you weren't sure you could successfully pull off a controlled draw or fade.

The point is, you face all kinds of different situations and make dozens of various swings every time you play.

The good news is that finding the Slot makes you better at executing each and every one. The Slot isn't only for full swings—it applies to half-swings, short swings, delicate swings around the green, and those that make the ball bend on command. The Slot is a shotmaking tool. Once you apply it to your full swing, try it out on the following specialty shots, and you'll save a few extra strokes every time you play.

Shot 1: The Burning Slot Wedge

How many times have you left an easy, 100-yard wedge shot short and right of the pin? Probably too many to remember. That's because the steep, over-the-top move that plagues your drives and approach shots also affects the short ones you hit with your wedges. The Burning Slot Wedge will get you back into the game.

The Burning Slot Wedge, unlike your high, weak floater, comes off the club with a low trajectory and tons of shot-stopping spin. It travels the same distance you normally hit your wedges but is much easier to control, especially if the wind is up or the pin is cut in the back portion of the green. You can hit it with each wedge you carry, including your lob wedge.

The lower, more penetrating ball flight you get with the Burning Slot Wedge makes it a versatile shot. Combining a steep backswing with the principles of the Slot guards against weak, soft hits that end up short of your target.

163

As with any shot, there are a few guidelines you must follow in order to produce a successful result:

1. Take your standard wedge address, but position the ball back in your stance, between the center and your right foot. This back-ball position encourages you to make a steep strike on the ball, instead of trying to help it into the air. It will feel as if you're squeezing the ball off the turf. Increase your left-hand grip pressure slightly. On my 1 to 10 scale, jack it up to 7 or 8.

2. As you take the club back, think about tracing a very narrow swing arc (wide is a killer). Lift your arms and hinge your wrists moderately, so that the clubhead gets higher than your hands at chest height. This steep backswing, combined with the back-ball position, encourages a solid, downward strike. Avoid taking the club back low to the ground at all costs. A low takeaway eliminates any chance of hitting a successful Burning Slot Wedge.

3. Once you reach the top of the backswing, drop the club to the inside as if you're making a full Slot Swing. Remember to start your forward motion with your lower body. Move it laterally and allow the clubhead to drag behind. This will increase your wrist setting, which is called down-cocking the club.

4. Keep your left-hand grip pressure firm as you swing down into impact. This helps you bow your left wrist so that the shaft leans toward the target at impact. Don't be afraid of the grass—take a nice, healthy divot. It helps if you keep both feet planted on the ground for this shot.

5. As you swing through the hitting zone, keep your hands and arms low and then pull them in close to your body. This is imperative for hitting a solid Burning Slot Wedge. If you swing your hands away from your body after impact, the ball will launch too high and land short of your target.

6. Make an abbreviated finish. A short follow-through promotes a lower trajectory and extra spin. The ball should land, hop twice, and then bite harder than a miner's handshake.

You must practice the Burning Slot Wedge before you try it out on the course. On the range, make a slow-motion backswing and downswing and stop at impact. Check that your hands are in front of the ball, your left wrist is firm and bowed, and your weight has shifted to your left foot. Hold your impact position for five seconds, and then repeat the drill ten times. Once you get these impact positions down pat, put the Burning Slot Wedge in your bag.

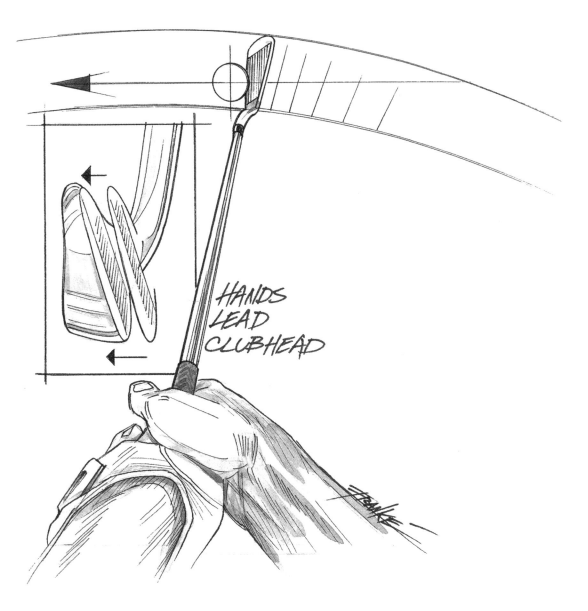

HANDS LEAD CLUBHEAD

Make sure your hands are in front of the ball and your left wrist is firm and bowed when hitting a Burning Slot Wedge.

Shot #2: The Slot Bunker Blast

Many instructors advocate swinging outside-to-inside to hit a bunker blast, and it's certainly one way to get the ball out of the sand. The problem is that amateurs tend to overdo the cut swing and don't swing with the speed necessary to hit anything but a short bunker shot. Also, the bunker blast requires that you contact the sand very near the ball, which makes it a very dangerous shot for the average golfer.

There's a better way: the Slot Bunker Blast. Believe it or not, Tiger Woods, Jim Furyk, Isao Aoki, Ken Venturi, and Lee Trevino (all of whom could be considered at the very top of the finest bunker players ever) loop the clubhead to the inside as they start their downswing when they blast the ball out of the sand.

I first learned the Slot Bunker Blast from Claude Harmon when I worked at Westchester Country Club in New York. Many top Tour pros came to Claude for bunker lessons, and I still consider his the best ever. Later, Claude's son, Butch, taught it to Tiger. The next time you catch Tiger on TV, see if he doesn't make the following moves when he hits a shot from a greenside bunker.

1. Address the ball with a *slightly* open stance (toe line pointed just left of the target). Play the ball just forward of center and position your hands so that the shaft doesn't lean toward the target. This keeps loft on the club and promotes an open clubface.

Slotting the club on your downswing will help you escape the sand more consistently than using the standard cut-shot approach.

168

2. Hinge the club up early in your takeaway, making sure to keep the clubface open and getting the clubhead above your hands as soon as possible. As you set the club, turn your shoulders back as in any other shot. If you do it correctly, the club will feel light and balanced.

3. Once you reach the top, make just a slight loop to the inside (using the Slot moves discussed throughout this book), but release the clubhead earlier than you do on normal swings. You need a ton of release to hit this shot correctly. Do not pull the clubhead.

4. As you reach the hitting zone, continue to release the club early and try to contact the sand three to four inches behind the ball. (Most teachers advocate hitting much closer to the ball, but the Slot Bunker Blast allows more room for error.) Pound that bunker with the flange of your sand wedge and continue through to your full finish.

With a little practice, you'll learn to pop the ball out beautifully. You'll be surprised at the height and power you get. If you have little room between you and the pin, rotate the clubface more open at address (to the right) and hold your follow-through short. For longer shots, swing to a full finish and hit closer to the ball. Regardless of the length of the shot you're trying to hit, always make an ample backswing. If you cut your backswing too short, you'll have a difficult time slotting the club, and you'll likely leave the ball in the sand.

Shot #3: The Slot Pitch and Chip

Over the years, I've played a lot of rounds with a fellow teaching professional named Carl Lohren. Carl wrote a top-selling instruction book called *One Move to Better Golf.* We played together often in the highly competitive Met Section. It seemed that he never shot higher than a 73 in the many competitive rounds we played, and he carded a lot of rounds in the 60s.

Back then, I'd often out-drive Carl by 80 yards. Carl was short off the tee but had one of the greatest short games I've ever seen. If he wasn't chipping or pitching the ball in the hole, he was knocking it so close you could just look at the ball and it would go in. His pitching and chipping were Tour-quality—no, better than that.

The more we played, the more attention I paid to his technique. It's amazing how a good short game can demoralize your opponents. I decided to fight fire with fire: I made a video of Carl's chipping technique and broke it down.

When I watched him onscreen, I saw the obvious: Carl slotted the club by making a slight inside loop on every pitch and chip, even the short ones. As I evolved in my teaching career, I began to notice that the best short-game players on Tour (i.e., Lee Trevino, Isao Aoki, Hubert Green, and, in recent times, Tiger Woods) slotted the club on short shots as well.

You wouldn't think that the Slot applied to delicate short shots around the green, but it does. I made the following observations while studying Carl's technique. Put them to use,

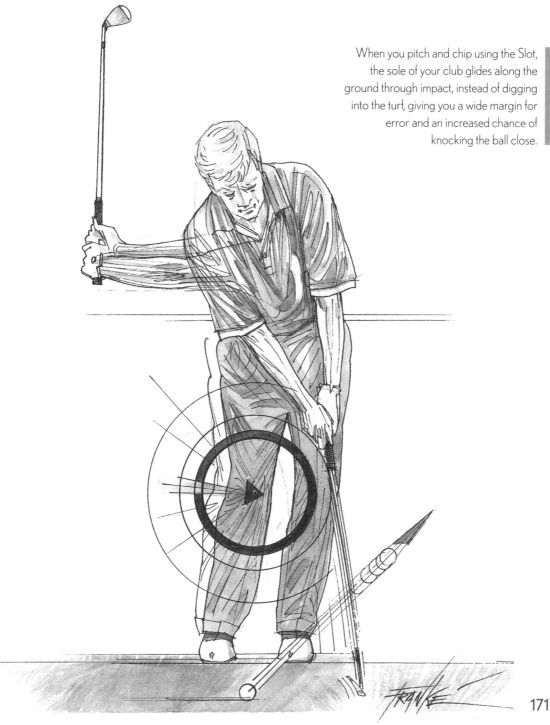

When you pitch and chip using the Slot, the sole of your club glides along the ground through impact, instead of digging into the turf, giving you a wide margin for error and an increased chance of knocking the ball close.

and you'll chip and pitch the ball closer than ever before (and demoralize a few opponents along the way).

Address

Set your weight over your front foot and take a narrow stance. Open your stance slightly by pulling your left foot back, and set the clubface square to your target. (You can open the clubface to hit a higher, softer chip, but remember—the more you open the face, the more you must open your stance.)

You should feel bent over at address with very relaxed shoulders, just as with the full Slot Swing.

Backswing

As you take the club back, try to swing it near the target line and keep the clubhead outside your hands. You should feel the clubhead lift off the ground early in your takeaway as it swings almost straight back. Keep your body super quiet and leave your weight over your left foot. This is basically a "hands-and-arms-only" backswing.

Transition

Once you reach the end of your backswing (which varies, depending on the length and the type of shot you're trying to hit), make a subtle loop back to the inside just as you do in a full Slot Swing, and be sure to incorporate a mini-shift and a turn through the ball. If you perform the move correctly, your left wrist will bend to a flat position and your right wrist will cup. *Caution*: If you do the subtle loop the wrong way, you'll kill any chance of making a successful shot.

Downswing

As you feel the club fall into the Slot, bring it into the back of the ball with your body active. Your body was quiet in your backswing, but now it helps power the shot. Once the club finds the Slot and is on plane, maintain the angle in your wrists and simply turn through.

Impact

Here's where the Slot Pitch and Chip get interesting. Most people assume that solid short shots are the result of striking down on the ball and digging the leading edge of the club-head into the turf. That's not the way Carl did it. Since your body's turn brings the clubhead into impact, your hands are not active. They don't throw or pull the clubhead. As a result, your club, shaft, and hands should form a fairly straight line through the hitting zone, with the sole of the club striking the turf. It should feel as if the clubhead is gliding across the ground, not digging into it.

Release

After impact, fight off releasing the club with your hands and instead hold the face square to your target. Resist like crazy! This allows you to hit the ball consistently straight at your target. A lot of amateurs have difficulty with this move, but a helpful tip is to rotate your head and follow the ball with your eyes after it leaves the clubface. It allows you to smoothly continue your turn through the ball. It's as if you're releasing with your eyes, not your clubhead.

If you do it correctly, your right wrist should feel slightly bent in your release. It's the exact same feeling as the one you get when you work a kid's paddle-ball game. Your right wrist is relaxed, but it never releases.

Shot #4: The Slot Fade

Swinging into impact following an inside track to the ball is counterintuitive to hitting a fade. Most fades result from swinging slightly out-to-in. So, yes, generating a left-to-right ball flight using the Slot (so that you can cut corners on dogleg-right holes or avoid trouble on the left side) takes a few adjustments. But for advanced players or those with Slot Swings so solid they can afford minor tweaks and deviations, the Slot Fade is a powerful weapon.

How powerful? Lee Trevino's brilliant career was based on

the Slot Fade. He used it to win six Majors and four scoring titles, as well as to beat Jack Nicklaus in an 18-hole playoff victory in the 1971 U.S. Open at Merion. Trevino had the good fortune to grow up in Dallas and study fellow Texan Ben Hogan. Trevino admired Hogan's swing. Check that—he *wanted* Hogan's swing. He tried to copy it, position by position, and generate the same level of ball-striking and Hogan's renowned power fade.

The problem is, Trevino couldn't do it, and in order to get the fade he so desperately wanted, he had to make some major changes. He couldn't stop hitting a low hook, so one of his adjustments was to aim as far left as possible and then underrelease the club and hit what amounted to a huge push fade.

To hit a Slot Fade as Trevino does, open your stance, drop into the Slot, and under-release the club through impact. Keep your left-hand knuckles pointing up after contact, with your left wrist slightly cupped at waist height in the finish. Don't roll your right hand over your left. When most golfers attempt this move, they end up quitting on the shot or blocking it out to the right—they confuse holding off the release with holding off the swing. If you look at old videotapes of Trevino, you'll notice that he drops his right shoulder and his arms straight down the same plane line, and he keeps his right side moving down the target line past impact and into his followthrough. One aspect of Trevino's swing that I've always loved was that it looks as if he's "gliding" into his finish. There's not an ounce of stoppage or hesitation in his swing.

Combining a slotted, inside approach to the ball with a fade release made Lee Trevino the most lethal and accurate Power Fader of his generation.

176

As previously mentioned, the Slot Fade is an advanced player's shot. The ideas are complex and are not intended for most golfers. Nonetheless, combining the Slot with what I call an under-release is a great way to hit a fade. And unlike other left-to-right ball flights, the Slot Fade comes with the proven power of an inside attack.

Shot #5: The Slot Draw

Most of the students attending my schools worldwide tell us they wish they could hit a draw. That's a commendable goal—and, when accomplished, it means they're achieving a better release, learning to make an inside attack track, and have a shot that rolls farther when it hits the ground for more distance.

The good news here is that following the principles of the Slot places you in a perfect position to hit the ball from right to left. The only way to produce a true draw that starts right of target and then moves gently toward it is to approach the ball from inside the target line and hit the inside quadrant of the ball. The Slot is all about an inside path.

One of the best Slot Drawers in history was Calvin Peete. Calvin is the all-time leader in Fairways Hit percentage (a category he led on Tour for ten straight years). He once went two years without missing a fairway at Muirfield Village during the Memorial Tournament.

Unlike Lee Trevino, who worked hard to hit a fade, drawing the ball came naturally to Peete. Amazingly, Calvin played his entire professional career with a fused left elbow (it had been set improperly after he broke it in three places in a childhood accident). It gave him a "short" left arm, making it easy for him to point his left elbow down at the ground during his backswing and set the shaft in a very vertical position on the way to the top.

After he completed his backswing, Peete made one of the best drop-down moves in the history of the game and slotted the club perfectly almost every time. I've studied his swing at length and can tell you that when his hands reached shoulder height in his downswing, his club was already behind his hands, with his right elbow noticeably below his left. He flattened the shaft dramatically.

Following the release of his right arm, his right wrist, and the clubshaft (the three Ls visible at the halfway-down point) through impact, Peete rotated his left arm so that his left elbow once again pointed at the ground, just as it did in his backswing. Pointing your left elbow at the ground in your follow-through like this is a very powerful and accurate action. When you do it correctly, it'll feel as if your right arm is very long and almost being pulled straight out of its socket. It also promotes an easy release where you don't have to focus so much attention on your hands or try to overwork them. These moves give you extension and a power release—the two important keys to hitting a draw.

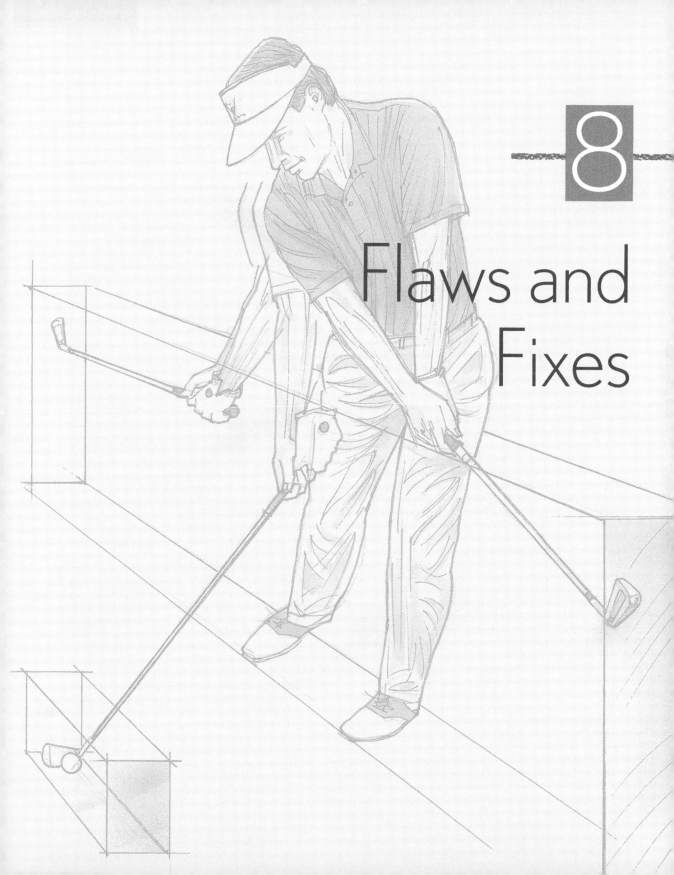

8

Flaws and Fixes

Even the best swings are prone to fall off-track. Yours is no exception. If you ever get to a position where you consistently find the Slot and then the feeling disappears, consult the flaws and the fixes below. They'll get you back in position in no time.

The Problem: Your Downswing Has Become Too Shallow

How You Know It's Happening

You're hitting a lot of hooks. When you're not hitting hooks, you're hitting behind the ball or catching it thin.

How to Fix It

It's not uncommon for an experienced Slot swinger to overdo it and get too shallow on the way back to the ball (what instructors describe as swinging the shaft "under plane"). Usually, these players confuse an "inside-out" swing path with the ideal swing arc. The perfect swing arc is actually inside, down the line, and then back to the inside (what I call the "Powerline Path").

To get back on plane and into the Slot, try the following drill:

1. Address an imaginary ball, swing to the top of your backswing, and stop. Now, swing down at 60 percent speed and stop when your hands reach hip height. As you do this, turn your hips more than you slide them, and don't let your arms fall behind your body (remember: your clubshaft flattens, not your arms).

2. Check that your shaft is parallel to the target line and not pointing to the right.

3. If it's not, start over. When you can get the shaft to sit parallel to the target line at the halfway-down delivery position (or on the *parallel target line*), reverse the move and swing back to your top position. Do this ten times or as many times as necessary for you to sense how your hands and arms work in concert with the shaft.

4. Swing to the halfway-through position, which should be a mirror image of the above. In other words, your clubshaft should again sit on the parallel target line. In order to do this, you must swing the club an equal amount back to the inside going through. When you do it, you've achieved my Powerline Idea!

If your swing becomes too shallow, make practice half-swings. Try to get your clubshaft to sit parallel to the target line at the halfway-back and halfway-through positions.

If you continue to have trouble, make sure you're not dropping your right shoulder backward or moving your head away from the target on your downswing. Try to feel as if you're more "on top" of the ball through impact.

The Problem: The Clubhead Is Getting "Stuck" behind Your Body

How You Know It's Happening

You feel as if you're "sweeping" the ball off the tee and hitting it well, but the sweeping feeling causes you to hit your irons and the fairway woods really thin and off to the right.

How to Fix It

Getting stuck is a term Tiger Woods has popularized, and a lot of golfers and instructors throw it around without knowing what *getting stuck* really means.

One way of getting stuck happens when you take the club back too far to the inside and establish a flat backswing plane, then try to slot the club on an even flatter plane on your downswing. The problem is, there isn't any room to further lower the plane. From the top, you're literally stuck. Keep in mind that this isn't what Tiger is talking about when he uses the same terminology (see "You're Over-using Your Lower Body" in the next section).

From this stuck position, the only thing you can do is flip your wrists at impact to square up the clubface; otherwise, you'll block the shot out to the right. This flip is very difficult to time and leads to very inconsistent ball-striking.

The correct fix is to either make your backswing more upright or change your downswing mechanics—as many great players do—and use the Reverse Slot.

To make your backswing steeper, go back to the reverse Figure-Eight Drill in chapter 6, and focus on swinging the clubhead out and away from you during your takeaway.

The Problem: You're Over-using Your Lower Body

How You Know It's Happening

You push the ball off to the right on one swing, then pull or severely hook the next (and vice versa).

How to Fix It

When your lower body fires too fast, the clubshaft can sometimes lie down or "drag" too much. This is a good player's problem—rarely do I see a weekend golfer with too much lower-body action. This is what Tiger Woods refers to when he talks about being stuck.

Good players tend to start down from a good backswing position with an explosive move, dramatically shifting and turning their lower bodies and hips. These quick and powerful lower-body moves can literally leave the arms and the hands in their tracks, setting them too far behind the turning action of the lower body. When the club reaches the delivery position (Step Five in my *Eight Step Swing* book and DVD), it's typically too far behind the hands and too far inside the target line.

If you ever find yourself in this situation, you'll immediately feel the need to reduce your body speed at impact so that your hands and clubhead can catch up. Like all compensating moves, this one is difficult to time, especially under pressure.

When Tiger isn't playing at his best, this is usually what's causing it. But when he says he's stuck, it's a problem that very few golfers ever face. This is because having the clubhead and the clubshaft behind your body as you begin your downswing isn't a "stuck" position. As you've read in this book, many great players swing down to the ball with a flat clubshaft and the clubhead well behind their bodies. The difference is that these players keep their left arms in close to their chests. When Tiger's arms and clubhead trail his body, he loses this important connection, an error caused by firing his hips too rapidly at the start of his downswing.

The Problem: Your Clubface Is Open at the Top of Your Backswing or at Impact or Both

How You Know It's Happening

You're hitting a lot of slices.

How to Fix It

In regular swings, an extremely open clubface at the top usually means an open clubface at the bottom and a heavy dose of slice-itis. In the Slot Swing, your clubface can be as open as you want it to be, but you'll need an extra move as you start back down.

I've copied this move from the Hall-of-Famer Mickey Wright, who won eighty-two LPGA tournaments before the age of thirty-four. Ben Hogan called Mickey's swing "the best I'd ever seen."

Mickey has written that she would "curl the last two fingers on my left hand downward" at the start of her downswing. This easy move is an excellent way to flatten your left wrist and square up the clubface for a powerful impact. It also does a good job of flattening out the shaft and dropping the clubhead into the Slot. I've used this idea hundreds of times with my students, usually with great results.

Practice Mickey's finger-curl for five minutes a day for a solid week. Don't even try to hit a ball. If you have access to a full-length mirror, place a piece of tape across it at a 45-degree angle. Set up with the mirror off to your right, swing to the top, make the Mickey move, and stop. Your clubshaft and clubface should match the angle made by the tape.

Curl the last two fingers of your left hand to rehearse proper
hand action at the start of the downswing. **189**

The Problem: Your Shaft Is Too Vertical in the Backswing

How You Know It's Happening

You rarely catch anything flush. Your contact frequently feels out toward the toe.

How to Fix It

Although the Slot Swing encourages a steep backswing, there's a danger in making it too steep. This happens when you pick up the clubhead without coiling your shoulders. It's this type of arm lift that makes your swing powerless.

To fix this problem, you need to incorporate an earlier turn. Try to tie your arms' swing with the turning action of your shoulders. This will feel like an exaggerated turn to an all-arms swinger, but it will quickly help you solve your steep backswing problems and allow you to hit much more powerful shots.

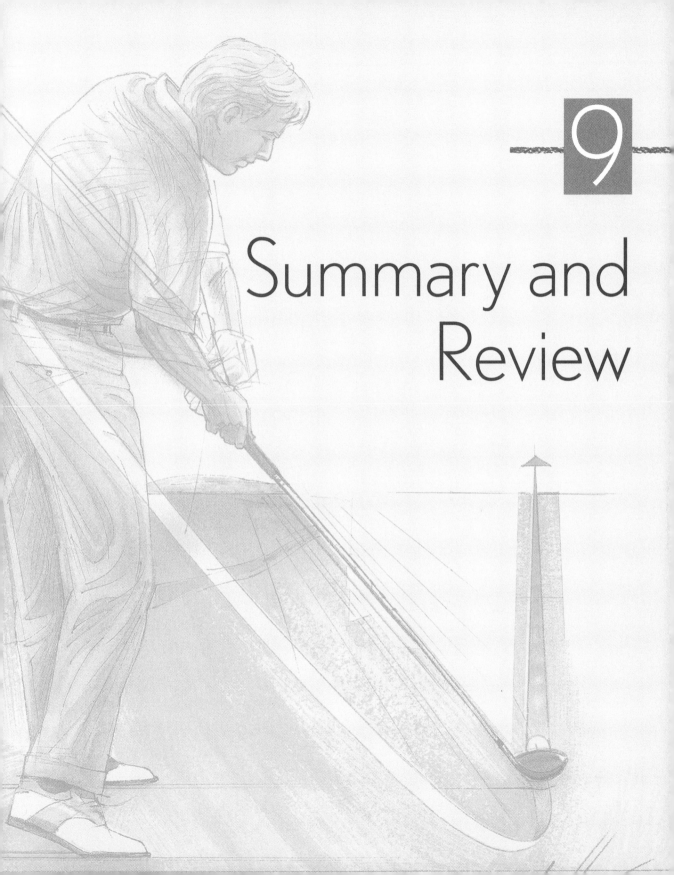

9

Summary and
Review

I hope this book has explained and vividly shown three possible swing shapes and how and why each one can work. I also hope you understand that there are multiple ways to make a backswing. I've lectured and written about the relative unimportance of a perfect backswing plane, the proof being that every single player on all professional tours takes the club to the top in his own unique way. Not one backswing is the same, even though so many teachers train their eyes on the backswing and teach rigid rules to every student they work with. For sure, the key to great ball-striking is in not tracing a precise path on the backswing or staying true to some imaginary perfect plane.

The truth is, there isn't a "one-plane" or a "two-plane" backswing. Each of your clubs is built with a different lie angle, and golfers come in all sizes, body types, and

coordination levels. Even hand shapes and sizes differ. So how can there be one correct plane? How could anyone look at the greatest ball-strikers in history and not see that all of their backswings were different?

It's much more important how you coil your body for efficiency and power. Then, it's all about how you start your downswing and whether you can repeat and find the Slot.

Most golfers have natural swing shape tendencies that can work great. They may not even know how these work. This book gives you many ways to see, feel, and understand the principles of the three swing shapes.

Is one shape better than another? Actually, they all work. It's up to you to decide which works best for your swing. At the very least, you're now armed with the ability to see and identify the various swings you see on the PGA Tour or on the range where you practice.

The secret to golf is hitting the Slot.